CONTEXTS
mathematics
FOR LEARNING

Beads and Shoes, Making Twos

Extending Number Sense

Madeline Chang
Catherine Twomey Fosnot

*first*hand
An imprint of Heinemann
A division of Reed Elsevier, Inc.
361 Hanover Street
Portsmouth, NH 03801–3912
firsthand.heinemann.com

Offices and agents throughout the world

ISBN 13: 978-0-325-01007-6
ISBN 10: 0-325-01007-2

Harcourt School Publishers
6277 Sea Harbor Drive
Orlando, FL 32887–6777
www.harcourtschool.com

ISBN 13: 978-0-15-360559-8
ISBN 10: 0-15-360559-6

 The development of a portion of the material described within was supported in part
by the National Science Foundation under Grant No. 9911841. Any opinions, findings,
and conclusions or recommendations expressed in these materials are those of the
authors and do not necessarily reflect the views of the National Science Foundation.

Library of Congress Cataloging-in-Publication Data
CIP data is on file with the Library of Congress

Printed in the United States of America on acid-free paper

11 10 09 08 07   ML   1 2 3 4 5 6

Acknowledgements

Literacy Consultant

Nadjwa E.L. Norton
Childhood Education, City College of New York

Photography

Herbert Seignoret
Mathematics in the City, City College of New York

Illustrator

Karen Pritchett

Schools featured in photographs

The Muscota New School/PS 314 (an empowerment school in Region 10), New York, NY
Independence School/PS 234 (Region 9), New York, NY
Fort River Elementary School, Amherst, MA

Contents

Unit Overview

This unit begins with the context of walking in line—two lines of children holding hands. The context encourages children to explore doubles while also strengthening their understanding of one-to-one correspondence. As the unit progresses, children explore containers that could hold doubles (such as egg cartons, English muffin packages, and juice boxes). Then the context shifts to an examination of pairs of shoes for varying numbers of people. As children investigate these situations, they explore both pairing and doubling—for instance, how six pairs of shoes can also be seen as six right shoes plus six left shoes (six sets of two or two sets of six). Later children work with greater numbers and the terminology of odds and evens is introduced.

In the second week, the story *Grandma's Necklaces* is used to develop a context for several investigations related to patterns made with two colors. The first necklace (one blue/one green repeating) can only be made with an even number of objects, because the unit that repeats has two objects. The second necklace (five blue/five green repeating) and the third necklace (three blue/three green repeating) challenge children to see a group of objects doubled as the unit that repeats.

The Landscape of Learning

BIG IDEAS

- Cardinality
- One-to-one correspondence
- Hierarchical inclusion
- Compensation and equivalence
- Unitizing
- Commutativity
- Patterns can be made from iterated units

STRATEGIES

- Using synchrony and one-to-one tagging
- Using trial and adjustment vs. systematic exploration
- Using doubles, near doubles, and compensation
- Counting three times vs. counting on
- Skip-counting

MODELS

- Arithmetic rack
- Open number line
- Bead string
- Hundred chart

Minilessons in the unit are crafted to support the automatizing of doubles and their use in solving near doubles—for example, using 6 + 6 to solve 6 + 7, or 10 + 10 to solve 9 + 10. Quick images and the arithmetic rack (see below) are both used with strings of related problems. The unit also includes the Shoe Game. This game can be played throughout the year for further support in developing the use of doubles as an addition strategy.

The Mathematical Landscape

The mathematical focus of this unit is early number sense. One of the manipulatives introduced in this unit is the arithmetic rack (the Dutch term is *rekenrek*) developed by Adri Treffers, a researcher at the Freudenthal Institute in the Netherlands. The rack is a calculating frame consisting of two rows of ten beads—two sets of five (one red and one white) in each row. (Instructions for making or buying your own arithmetic rack are included on page 61.)

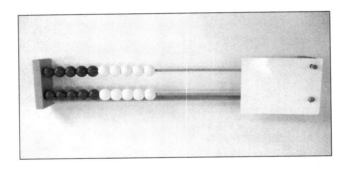

Based on much developmental research, the arithmetic rack was designed to align with children's early number sense strategies, enabling them to move from counting one by one to decomposing and composing numbers with subunits (Treffers 1991). It encourages the use of strategies such as doubles and near doubles for the basic facts, whereas counters alone are likely to keep children at the stage of counting by ones. The unit also introduces children to odd and even numbers and promotes development of a strong sense of doubles and pairing.

BIG IDEAS

This unit is designed to encourage the development of some of the big ideas underlying early number sense:

❖ *cardinality*

❖ *one-to-one correspondence*

❖ *hierarchical inclusion*

❖ *compensation and equivalence*

❖ *unitizing*

❖ *commutativity*

❖ *patterns can be made from iterated units*

❖ *Cardinality*

Young children often count by rote without understanding the purpose of counting. They may not have constructed the big idea of cardinality—that the number they end on is the number of objects in the set. Thus, it is important when children finish counting to ask, "So how many do you have?" Don't assume that because they seem to count well they understand that 8 means eight objects. They may think the eighth object is 8.

❖ *One-to-one correspondence*

One-to-one correspondence requires that children understand that if there are two groups, and if each object in one group is paired with an object in the other group, then the groups have the same number of objects.

❖ *Hierarchical inclusion*

Even when children do understand cardinality and one-to-one correspondence, they still may not realize that the numbers grow by one, and exactly one, each time. Researchers call this idea hierarchical inclusion (Kamii 1985). They mean that amounts nest inside each other: six includes five, plus one; five includes four, plus one, etc. This idea underlies the strategy of using doubles to solve near-doubles problems. For example, to use 6 + 6 to solve 6 + 7, children need to understand that there is one more than 6 in the 7.

❖ Compensation and equivalence

Children may initially have a difficult time comprehending that 5 + 3 is equivalent to 4 + 4. The big ideas here are compensation and equivalence—that if you lose one (from the five, for example) but gain it (onto the three), the total stays the same. These big ideas, once constructed, allow children to realize that a problem like 6 + 8 can be solved with the double 7 + 7.

❖ Unitizing

Unitizing requires that children use numbers to count not only objects but also groups—and to count them both simultaneously. For young learners, unitizing is a shift in perspective. Children have just learned to count ten objects, one by one. Unitizing these ten things as *one* thing—one group—challenges their original idea of number. How can something be ten and one at the same time?

❖ Commutativity

Commutativity for addition can be represented algebraically as $a + b = b + a$ and for multiplication, as $a \times b = b \times a$. Children need many opportunities to compose and decompose numbers before they come to realize that numbers can be grouped in a variety of ways, even turned around, and the amounts stay the same. Underlying an understanding of doubles is the idea that each object is paired with another. As children explore the pairing and doubling in a variety of contexts, they come to understand that doubles can be thought of as a group of pairs, as well as an amount doubled, $6 \times 2 = 2 \times 6$.

❖ Patterns can be made from iterated units

Psychologists have shown that even toddlers can recognize simple repeating patterns (Dehaene 1999). However, *reproducing* patterns is a different matter and can be quite a challenge for kindergarteners and even first graders. Reproducing a pattern requires unitizing—the objects in the group must be seen as a unit that will be repeated (iterated). A pattern of five blue beads and five green beads iterated over and over is not just ten beads. It is two sets of five in alternating colors. The five is a set—a unit—and two sets of five are also a unit!

As you work with the activities in this unit, you will see children using many strategies to determine amounts. Here are some strategies to notice:

❖ **using synchrony and one-to-one tagging**

❖ **counting three times vs. counting on**

❖ **using trial and adjustment vs. systematic exploration**

❖ **skip-counting**

❖ **using doubles, near doubles, and compensation**

❖ Using synchrony and one-to-one tagging

Counting effectively requires children to coordinate many actions simultaneously. Not only must they remember the word that comes next, they must use only one word for each object (synchrony) and tag each object once and only once (one-to-one tagging). When children are first learning to count, this coordination is very difficult; they often skip some objects, double-tag others, and are not synchronized, using too many or too few words for the number of objects they are counting.

❖ Counting three times vs. counting on

Making groups and determining the total number of objects in them is also a challenge for children. To determine whether arrangements work, they may tediously count three times—first each of the two groups and then the whole, starting from one each time. For example, to see how many children there are in two lines of 8 children each, they may count 1 through 8 twice and then count from 1 to 16. A major landmark strategy to notice and celebrate is when a child begins to count on—labeling the first set 8 and then continuing: "9, 10, . . . 16."

❖ Using trial and adjustment vs. systematic exploration

Often children begin to solve a problem using trial and error. A major change to celebrate occurs when they begin to use the results of an attempt at a solution to adjust their strategy. For example, as they try to find a size that works for one of the patterns of necklaces, they may randomly select numbers to try. When one doesn't work, they may add or remove beads. As they find several numbers that work, they will begin to generalize and their approach will become less random. Some children will eventually systematically generate possibilities with numbers alone as they begin to realize the patterns evolving with the numbers.

❖ Skip-counting

At first skip-counting can be rote. Children know the singsong "2, 4, 6" or "10, 20, 30." But they often do not take an appropriately matching group. They say two and only tag one. The contexts in this unit are designed to support skip-counting. The first contexts are familiar containers, or pairs of children in line, or pairs of shoes. Later in the unit they are the groups of beads in necklaces.

❖ Using doubles, near doubles, and compensation

A great way to help children automatize the basic addition and subtraction facts is to work on relationships. For example, by itself $7 + 6$ can be a difficult fact to learn, but when it is explored in relation to a double such as $7 + 7$ or $6 + 6$ it is easier. Once the doubles are known, they can be used for many other problems: $5 + 7 = 6 + 6$, $7 + 3 = 5 + 5$, and $7 + 6 = 6 + 6 + 1$ (or $7 + 7 - 1$), etc.

MATHEMATICAL MODELING

Several models are used in this unit: the arithmetic rack, the open number line, the bead string, and the hundred chart. Models go through three stages of development (Gravemeijer 1999; Fosnot and Dolk 2001):

❖ *model of the situation*

❖ *model of children's strategies*

❖ *model as a tool for thinking*

❖ Model of the situation

The context of walking in line in two rows is introduced and then modeled in a minilesson on the arithmetic rack. The total numbers of children in the rows are labeled as doubles and placed on a number line, which children build themselves. The bead string (as represented by the necklaces) also lends itself to an understanding of a number line representation of quantity. The hundred chart, which (in contrast to the number line) has a ten-structure built in, is introduced as a chart to mark necklace sizes.

❖ Model of children's strategies

Once the models have been introduced to represent the situation, you can use them to model children's strategies as they determine arrangements. The arithmetic rack can be used to model double and near-double strategies and compensation by sliding over beads. If a child counts by ones, move one bead at a time; if a child counts on, move the beginning set and then move beads one at a time onto the set. If a child uses compensation, remove a bead from one group and slide another bead to the other group. The number line with the doubles can be used to represent addition and subtraction. If you start on a double and subtract one, you land between two doubles. But if you subtract two, you land on another double. A bead string with an AB pattern using two colors can be used similarly. Moving down and across on the hundred chart can be used to represent skip-counting and the addition of groups.

❖ Model as a tool for thinking

Eventually children will be able to use these models as tools for thinking—they will be able to imagine $6 + 4$ being shown to be equivalent to $5 + 5$ on the arithmetic rack. The bead string will become a helpful image for odd and even numbers. Over time, the arithmetic rack can become an important model to support children in learning the basic facts for addition and subtraction (Treffers 1991); the open number line will become particularly helpful for addition and subtraction; and the hundred chart can be helpful in exploring patterns in the number system.

Many opportunities to discuss these landmarks in mathematical development will arise as you work through the unit. Look for moments of puzzlement. Don't hesitate to let children discuss their ideas or check and recheck their counting. Celebrate their accomplishments! These are developmental milestones.

A graphic of the full landscape of learning for early number sense, addition, and subtraction is provided on page 10. The purpose of this graphic is to allow you to see the longer journey of children's mathematical development and to place your work with this unit within the scope of this long-term development. You may also use this graphic as a helpful way to record the progress of individual children for yourself. Each landmark can be shaded in as you find evidence in a child's work and in what the child says—evidence that the child has constructed the landmark strategies and big ideas. In a sense, you will be recording the individual pathways children take as they develop as young mathematicians.

References and Resources

Bemelmans, Ludwig. 1958. *Madeline*. New York, NY: Viking.

Dehaene, Stanislas. 1999. *The Number Sense: How the Mind Creates Mathematics*. New York, NY: Oxford University Press.

Dolk, Maarten, and Catherine Twomey Fosnot. 2004a. *Addition and Subtraction Minilessons, Grades PreK–3*. CD-ROM with accompanying facilitator's guide by Antonia Cameron, Sherrin B. Hersch, and Catherine Twomey Fosnot. Portsmouth, NH: Heinemann.

———. 2004b. *Fostering Children's Mathematical Development, Grades PreK–3: The Landscape of Learning*. CD-ROM with accompanying facilitator's guide by Sherrin B. Hersch, Antonia Cameron, and Catherine Twomey Fosnot. Portsmouth, NH: Heinemann.

Fosnot, Catherine Twomey, and Maarten Dolk. 2001. *Young Mathematicians at Work: Constructing Number Sense, Addition, and Subtraction*. Portsmouth, NH: Heinemann.

Gravemeijer, Koeno P. E. 1999. How emergent models may foster the constitution of formal mathematics. *Mathematical Thinking and Learning* 1 (2): 155–77.

Kamii, Constance. 1985. *Young Children Reinvent Arithmetic*. New York: Teachers College Press.

Treffers, Adri. 1991. Rekenen tot twentig met het rekenrek [Calculating to twenty with the arithmetic rack]. *Willem Bartjens* 10 (1): 35–45.

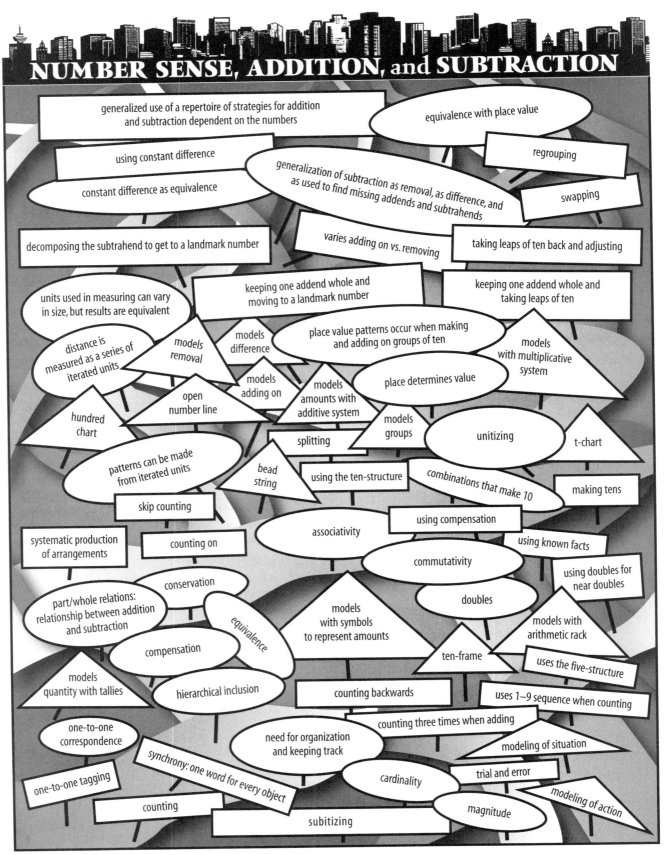

The landscape of learning: number sense, addition, and subtraction on the horizon showing landmark strategies (rectangles), big ideas (ovals), and models (triangles).

DAY ONE
Walking in Line

The context of walking hand in hand in two lines is used to explore doubling. This context is familiar to most children because many classes walk in line this way. You can also use the classic children's book *Madeline* by Ludwig Bemelmans to develop the context. Children then draw different size groups (placed in lines) to produce doubles. For example, with a line of four, how many children will there be altogether in two such lines? This can be represented as 4 + 4; then consider a line of five (5 + 5), a line of six (6 + 6), etc. The context also supports one-to-one correspondence (each child walks in line with a partner, so each line has the same number of children). Children draw possible numbers of walking partners and then discuss strategies they found helpful in a short math congress.

Day One Outline

Developing the Context

☀ Introduce the context of walking in two lines and ask children to investigate different doubling scenarios.

Supporting the Investigation

☀ Note children's strategies as they record different doubling scenarios and use the context to help children realize the meaning of what they are doing.

Preparing for the Math Congress

☀ Plan to scaffold a congress discussion that will support the development of more efficient strategies.

Facilitating the Math Congress

☀ Discuss a range of different strategies and explore why the strategies work.

Materials Needed

Madeline by Ludwig Bemelmans *(optional)*

Connecting cubes, plastic teddy bears, or other counters, as needed

Drawing paper—a few sheets per child

Large chart pad and easel (or chalkboard or whiteboard)

Markers

Developing the Context

☀ Introduce the context of walking in two lines and ask children to investigate different doubling scenarios.

Explain to the children that you have been thinking that walking in two lines might be helpful when the class goes somewhere. Have 3 children stand up in a line and ask, "If we make another line of 3, how many children would that be in all?" Record this as $3 + 3 = 6$. Try this again with a different number, such as 5. Have 5 children stand in a line and ask the class to consider how many children would be in line if another group of 5 is formed; then record $5 + 5 = 10$. (Or you can read Madeline. After you finish reading the story, reread the first two pages:"In an old house in Paris that was covered in vines, lived 12 little girls in two straight lines." Often children notice that the little girls are walking in line"just like we do!"Ask the class to figure out how many little girls are walking in each line and record that as $6 + 6 = 12$.)

After you have developed the context of walking in two lines, encourage children to think about different numbers. What if there were 7 children in each line? What would the total be? If there were 8 in each line, what would the total be then? What about this class? How many would be in each line— and would everyone have a partner? (If there is an odd number of children in the class, you can become the singleton's partner.) What if someone is absent? What if 2 people are absent? Ask the children to work individually at tables and investigate.

Supporting the Investigation

☀ Note children's strategies as they record different doubling scenarios and make use of the context to help children realize the meaning of what they are doing.

Have manipulatives like connecting cubes, counters, or plastic teddy bears available for children who need to make a concrete representation of the numbers and context. Pass out drawing paper so children can make their own record of the different scenarios they are trying. Drawing two sets of the same number of objects may not be easy for some children. Providing blank paper as opposed to grid paper allows children to grapple with the concept of one-to-one correspondence and to come up with their own solutions to the problem (see Inside One Classroom, page 13). As children work, walk around and take note of the challenges and strategies you see them dealing with.

Conferring with Children at Work

Josie: I'm making lines with the teddy bears, first, and then I'm drawing the children. *(Josie makes two lines of objects. One line is longer and has more.)*

Madeline (the teacher): I see that you are making beautiful lines, Josie. But I'm wondering...one of your lines looks longer than the other. How do you know that everyone in this line has a partner in the other line?

Josie: *(Looks puzzled at first and then figures out a solution.)* I know! We have to hold hands with our partners. I can draw them holding hands! *(Places the plastic teddy bears in two rows on the drawing paper and makes pairs by drawing a line from each bear in one row to the corresponding bear in the other row, to represent children holding hands with their partners.)* I need one more teddy bear here.

Madeline: How many do you have in each row now?

Josie: I have 1, 2, 3, 4, 5, 6, 7. So I have 7!

Madeline: And how many in this line?

Josie: Also 7! See, they're holding hands now.

Madeline: I see. That was a great idea. So shall we record this one as 7 plus 7? How many children is that?

Josie: 1, 2, ... 14. *(Counts by ones to 14.)* How do you write that?

Madeline: *(Writes 14 for her.)* Like this—14. Wow! You found another special double number.

Author's Notes

Many children will draw one line of objects first and then complete the second line. It is sometimes a struggle for children to draw two corresponding sets of the same number of objects, and they might draw the second line of children longer or shorter than the first line. Madeline makes use of the context. Staying in the context helps children realize the meaning of what they are doing and may create conditions for them to develop their own solutions. It can help them develop an understanding of one-to-one correspondence and doubling.

Madeline checks first to see if Josie realizes that the number in each line is the same; then she asks for a total.

How a number is represented is social knowledge—a label or name—and does not need to be constructed in the same way as a mathematical idea. Madeline shows Josie how to make the numerals and then celebrates the finding of another double.

Preparing for the Math Congress

As children work, note the various challenges they encounter and the strategies they use. Here are some strategies you will probably see:

* Drawing lines of children with the two lines not equal in number. Here the challenge is cardinality and one-to-one correspondence. As you confer, ask how many children are in each line and if everyone has a partner. Stay grounded in the context to help children realize the meaning of what they are doing.

☀ Plan to scaffold a congress discussion that will support the development of more efficient strategies.

- Double-tagging or skipping objects as they count. Here the challenge is counting. Ask children to double-check and to consider how they might keep track.

- Counting on from the first line. Some children may count on when adding. For example, to add 6 + 6, they may say 7, 8, 9, 10, 11, and 12.

- Children who have not constructed counting on will usually need to count three times to produce the total: first the objects in one line, then the objects in the second line, then the total number in both lines, starting from one.

- Skip-counting by twos. Children who see the children in the lines paired (since they are holding hands) may try skip-counting by twos.

- Using a known double to calculate a new one. For example, to calculate 6 + 6, children might use 5 + 5 and then add 2. Or to calculate 9 + 9, they might use 10 + 10 and subtract 2.

After children have had a sufficient amount of time to work, bring everyone back to the meeting area to discuss the strategies they have found useful.

▨ Tips for Structuring the Math Congress

Look for a few different, yet prevalent challenges and the way children have found solutions. For example, if several children have struggled to count, you might ask a child who figured out a nice way to keep track to share first. If most children are counting three times but a few have begun to count on, you might have them share how they counted on and ask the group to consider if and why the counting on strategy works. Lastly, if some children have noticed that the pairs can be used to skip-count, you can ask them to share this strategy and explore why it works with the community.

Facilitating the Math Congress

☀ Discuss a range of different strategies and explore why the strategies work.

Ask the children to come to the meeting area to discuss strategies they found helpful. Have their work folders handy, so after the congress the work can be stored in their folders for use on Day Two.

A Portion of the Math Congress

Author's Notes

Madeline (the teacher): As I walked around, I saw everybody using so many wonderful strategies. We found lots of doubles, didn't we? And it was hard to draw all of these lines and to count and keep track. Josie, you found a great way to make sure the number of kids was the same in each line, didn't you? Would you share what you did?

Madeline begins by framing the problem—how to keep track—and then invites Josie to explain a solution.

Josie: I made everybody hold hands. Then I knew everybody had a partner. *(Josie displays her drawing of 7 + 7 showing how pairs are holding hands.)* And then I counted. *(Counts from 1 to 14.)*

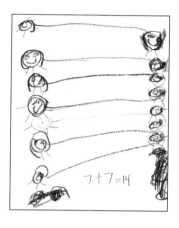

Madeline: And I saw so many ways to count, too. Brian, do you think you could use Josie's picture to explain to everyone how you counted? There are 7 kids in this line. *(Covers one line with her hand.)* So how many all together?

By using Josie's picture and covering a line of seven, Madeline provides a constraint on the "counting three times" strategy. The initial group is now hidden and cannot be counted by ones.

Brian: 8, 9, 10, 11, 12, 13, 14.

Madeline: That was fast! Why didn't Brian start at one? Turn to the person sitting next to you and talk about that. Why did Brian start counting at 8? *(After a few minutes of pair talk, the conversation resumes.)* Josie?

By providing pair talk and returning to Josie, Madeline challenges her to make sense of a counting on strategy.

Josie: Because he already knew that part.

Madeline: So if we know this part is 7 we don't need to count it again? Wow. That's a great shortcut, isn't it? Thanks for sharing that, Brian. Some of you might want to try Brian's idea when we work on this some more later. Yolanda, you figured out a great way to count, too. Come show your way.

Yolanda: I went 2, 4, 6, 8, 10, 12, 14. *(Points to each pair with two fingers.)*

Madeline: So what if you had 8 and 8?

Josie's picture also provides a nice representation for Yolanda to use in order to share skip-counting.

Yolanda: That would be 2 more. That's 16!

Assessment Tips

Note which children do not use one-to-one correspondence and have drawn unequal lines. Observe the counting strategies and note who needs to count over and over again to be certain the amount is still the same; who counts three times; who counts on; and who skip-counts. Do any children use known doubles to figure out unknown doubles? It is helpful to jot down your observations on sticky notes. Later, these can be placed on children's drawings to be included in their portfolios.

Sample Children's Work

One-to-one correspondence is not yet evident. The child has drawn several children in two lines but not all have partners.

Shows one-to-one correspondence with a total of fourteen children.

One double is used to calculate another.

Reflections on the Day

Today, children were introduced to the context of walking in line with partners and they determined a variety of doubles. You were able to see who is still struggling with one-to-one correspondence. You also were able to support the development of counting by twos and to help children see the relationship between counting by twos and doubling. On Day Two, children will continue with this work and you will hold a more extensive math congress to discuss the relationship between pairing and doubles.

Recording Doubles on the Number Line

Today, the math workshop begins with a minilesson—a string of related problems using doubles shown as quick images, on the class-size arithmetic rack. Children are reminded of the helpful strategies shared on Day One and then they continue with the work of finding more doubles. In the math congress the doubles are posted on an open number line that is then compared to a standard number line in order to explore how doubling is also connected to counting by twos.

Day Two Outline

Minilesson: Quick Images

☀ Show and discuss quick image arrangements of beads on the arithmetic rack designed to support children in automatizing doubles and using doubles to solve near-doubles problems.

Developing the Context

☀ Have children work with partners to share their strategies and explore more doubles.

Supporting the Investigation

☀ Support children in developing more efficient strategies.

Preparing for the Math Congress

☀ Ask children to make lists of all the doubles they have found.

☀ Prepare a paper strip to be used as an open number line.

Facilitating the Math Congress

☀ Record on chart paper the doubles children found and use the children's drawings or the arithmetic rack to illustrate their thinking.

☀ Record the numbers on the paper strip and the corresponding expressions on index cards.

☀ Encourage children to notice patterns in the numbers and to compare the paper strip open number line to a standard number line.

Materials Needed

Class-size arithmetic rack, with cover-up board

Instructions for making an arithmetic rack can be found in Appendix A. Visit contextsforlearning.com for information on where to purchase an arithmetic rack.

Connecting cubes, plastic teddy bears, or other counters, as needed

Children's work from Day One

Drawing paper—a few sheets per group of two or three children

Long strip of paper or roll of adding machine paper

3" by 5" index cards— one pack

A standard number line

Large chart pad and easel

Markers

Minilesson: Quick Images (10–15 minutes)

☀ Show and discuss quick image arrangements of beads on the arithmetic rack designed to support children in automatizing doubles and using doubles to solve near-doubles problems.

Use the class-size arithmetic rack to flash various quick images of arrangements of beads—symbolizing children standing in two parallel lines. Show the arrangement for only a few seconds, then use the cover-up board or a piece of fabric to cover the image. Each time you show an image, ask, "How many kids (beads) are in line?" and "How do you know?" Invite discussion on several strategies. Support children in developing strategies to automatize doubles and to use doubles for near-doubles problems.

Behind the Numbers

Three is an amount that most children can see as a unit (subitize); it is not likely that they will need to count. The string starts there to support the use of counting on (from 3) or, if the double is known, to use it to solve the problems that come next. The first three problems are tightly sequenced so as to generate a conversation on how each line gains one, but the total number in both lines gains two. This is a nice place to revisit a conversation on a skip-counting strategy if one was shared and discussed on Day One. The total number of beads in the fourth problem is one less than the total of the previous problem and is not a double, but either 4 + 4 or 5 + 5 can be helpful in solving it. This fact is important to discuss, as it will encourage children to use doubles to figure out near doubles. In the last two problems, 10 + 10 is also often a known fact that children can use to figure out the sum of 9 + 9.

String of related quick images:

3 on the top, 3 on the bottom

4 on the top, 4 on the bottom

5 on the top, 5 on the bottom

5 on the top, 4 on the bottom

10 on the top, 10 on the bottom

9 on the top, 9 on the bottom

Developing the Context

After the minilesson, remind children of the wonderful, helpful strategies they shared on Day One and suggest that they try to use some of those strategies today. Distribute children's work from Day One and additional sheets of drawing paper. Have children work in pairs or small groups so they can share the strategies they try and the numbers they find that are doubles.

Supporting the Investigation

☀ Support children in developing more efficient strategies.

Move around the room noting the strategies that children are using. Support them in developing strategies today that are more efficient than those they used on Day One. Encourage them to make use of a previous problem to solve a new one by building onto doubles they know. Ask them to reflect on the following questions:

✦ How many did they have in each line?

✦ How did they figure out the total number in the class?

✦ Is there a strategy they found helpful?

✦ Can they use one solution to help with another?

Preparing for the Math Congress

Ask children to look back over all their work from today and Day One and make a list of the doubles they found. For example, have them use their pictures to record just the totals. From a cross-section of the class, you should get a fairly nice list to discuss in the math congress. The congress today will be used to get these even numbers up on an open number line and to discuss any patterns the children notice. In preparation for the congress, tape a long strip of adding machine paper on the chalkboard (or below it, or on a wall where there is substantial room to also hang index cards and children's drawings). You will use this strip to create an open number line. *[See Figure 1]*

* Ask children to make lists of all the doubles they have found.

* Prepare a paper strip to be used as an open number line.

Figure 1

Facilitating the Math Congress

Convene the children in the meeting area to discuss the doubles they found. Make a list on chart paper as children share, checking each suggested scenario out with either a child's drawing or the class-size arithmetic rack. After the list is complete, ask which shows the least number of children. Mark a vertical line on the paper strip and write the corresponding expression on an index card—for example, $1 + 1$, for 2. For now just mark the numbers they have found. As you progress with marking the doubles on the paper strip, children will probably begin noticing patterns and they will conjecture about new doubles for the list. This is precisely the point of building the number line—not only as a representation of their work, but also as a tool. You might find it helpful at points in the conversation to refer to the standard number line, asking the children to compare and share what they notice about these two different number lines. Most children will notice that the standard number line has numbers going up by ones whereas the open number line that the class is making skips every other number. They may also notice that all the numbers on the open number line end in 0, 2, 4, 6, or 8, whereas the numbers in between (those not listed on the open number line) end in 1, 3, 5, 7, and 9. If they have explored the number of children in their own class when children are absent, you can use the open number line to show what happens when one is subtracted, or two, etc. Interesting generalities can be made regarding the numbers subtracted, depending on whether your class size is even or odd. For example, subtracting an odd number from an odd number produces an even number; subtracting an even number from an even number produces an even number; etc.

* Record on chart paper the doubles children found and use the children's drawings or the arithmetic rack to illustrate their thinking.

* Record the numbers on the paper strip and the corresponding expressions on index cards.

* Encourage children to notice patterns in the numbers and to compare the paper strip open number line to a standard number line.

Author's Notes

Madeline (the teacher)**:** So we have a lot of numbers on our chart. Let's start posting them on this strip, like a number line. *(Pointing to the standard number line posted nearby.)* I wonder which of these is the smallest. Where shall we begin? Mathew?

Mathew: I did 3 plus 3. It's 6.

It is common that children will not see one plus one as a possibility because they don't think of one child as a "line."

Madeline: *(Pushes 3 red beads over on the top of the arithmetic rack and 3 red beads over on the bottom.)* Do we agree that 3 plus 3 is 6? *(Some children count and then nod.)* OK. Let's post your record.

Madeline does not acknowledge the answer as correct. Instead she turns to the community for consensus. Since the numbers are small in magnitude, the children can easily imagine them.

Leah: It's not the littlest though. I think we could do 2 and 2. That's 4.

Madeline: Shall we add that one? *(Many children nod, so it is added.)* Daniel, you tried a different number. What did you find out?

Daniel: I found out that 4 plus 4 equals 8.

Madeline: How shall I make that on the arithmetic rack?

Daniel: One more on top and one more on the bottom.

Madeline: So 3 plus 3 was 6, and now 4 plus 4 is 8. This reminds me of our minilesson!

Sophie: Two more.

Madeline: Isn't that interesting? Two more.

Madeline notes the importance of what Sophie has noticed and emphasizes it by repeating it.

Sadie: I counted by twos. *(Holds her drawing of 14 children in 2 lines.)* See, 2, 4, 6, 8, 10, 12, 14. It's 7 and 7 in a line. If it's 8 kids, it would just be 2 more.

(Several more numbers go up.)

CJ: Hey. *(Pointing to the standard number line.)* That one over there is going up like this—1, 2, 3, 4, 5—and ours is 2, 4, 6, 8…

By placing the standard number line nearby, Madeline supports children in noticing similarities and differences in the lines.

Daniel: It's like Sadie counting by twos.

Reflections on the Day

The children had an opportunity today to explore several numbers and to double them. Quick images encouraged them to use solutions for one problem to help solve others by "building on" in twos. After finding more doubles, they began to construct an open number line to represent the results of their doubling. As they compared this to a traditional number line, they noticed the difference of two between each pair of consecutive points. Although not all children are expected to understand fully why this is happening, they are developing strategies that will help in automatizing the doubles and in making use of them for solving other addition problems.

DAY THREE

Things That Come in Doubles

The day begins with another minilesson—a string of related problems using doubles and near doubles. This string is not worked through using quick images because the numbers involved are difficult to subitize at a quick glance. After the minilesson, children are asked to consider where else they might have seen doubles in the world around them and to design containers for other larger numbers of objects that are also doubles. Children make posters of their designs and discuss them in a math congress.

Materials Needed

Class-size arithmetic rack

Containers of things that come in doubles (even numbers), such as juice boxes, English muffin packages, or egg cartons of various sizes

Drawing paper—a few sheets per child

Large chart paper—one sheet per child

Connecting cubes, plastic teddy beards, or other counters, as needed

Pocket hundred chart with numeral cards and transparent colored inserts

Open number line from Day Two

Markers

Day Three Outline

Minilesson: A String of Related Problems

☀ Show and discuss arrangements of beads on the arithmetic rack designed to support children in automatizing doubles and using doubles to solve near-doubles problems.

Developing the Context

☀ Facilitate a discussion about a variety of containers that hold doubles.

☀ Ask children to design new sizes of containers for larger doubles.

Supporting the Investigation

☀ Note children's strategies and encourage them to articulate their thinking.

Preparing for the Math Congress

☀ Ask children to make posters of their work and then conduct a "gallery walk" to give them a chance to review each other's posters.

Facilitating the Math Congress

☀ Use a pocket hundred chart to highlight the sizes of containers children made.

☀ Encourage children to notice the patterns that appear and to use those patterns to predict other numbers that might be doubles.

Minilesson: A String of Related Problems (10–15 minutes)

Use the class-size arithmetic rack to complete the following string. Show one problem at a time on the arithmetic rack. Each time you show an image, state the problem and ask for thumbs-up when children have an answer. Explore alternative strategies but encourage the children to make use of the relations in the string.

☀ Show and discuss arrangements of beads on the arithmetic rack designed to support children in automatizing doubles and using doubles to solve near-doubles problems.

String of related problems:

3 on the top, 3 on the bottom

5 on the top, 5 on the bottom

5 on the top, 6 on the bottom

8 on the top, 8 on the bottom

7 on the top, 8 on the bottom

6 on the top, 6 on the bottom

7 on the top, 6 on the bottom

Behind the Numbers

Children probably just know the solutions to the first two problems. The second problem can be used to solve the third. The fourth problem might be more challenging and many children may resort to counting by ones, but you can encourage them to think about whether any of the previous problems can be helpful. For example, the first two problems can be used: (5 + 5) + (3 + 3). The color of the beads on the arithmetic rack makes these doubles stand out. The string continues with more doubles and near doubles. Encourage children to use a known double to solve an unknown near double.

Developing the Context

Remind children of the doubles they put on the number line on Day Two and ask them to consider other examples of doubles in the world around them. For instance, the different numbers of juice boxes packaged together may be a familiar context for a class that has snack time every day. English muffins come in two sets of three; larger packages have two sets of six. One class working with this unit was hatching chicks and they noticed that the configuration of the egg cartons that the fertile eggs had come in was 6 + 6, holding a total of a dozen eggs. Their investigation began with the cartons most familiar to consumers: cartons for six, eight, and twelve eggs.

After a preliminary discussion of a variety of containers that hold doubles, ask children to design new sizes. For example, if you decide to explore egg cartons, have a variety of sizes on hand. Ask the children to share what they notice about the design of the carton and how many eggs each carton will hold. Then ask them to think about what other sizes of egg cartons there might be. Show them the carton for six eggs and eight eggs and ask them why they think there is not a carton for seven eggs. What other numbers would work for egg cartons? How many eggs would a 10 + 10 carton hold? How about one with a 13 + 13 configuration?

☀ Facilitate a discussion about a variety of containers that hold doubles.

☀ Ask children to design new sizes of containers for larger doubles.

Supporting the Investigation

Note children's strategies and encourage them to articulate their thinking.

After discussion, give each child some drawing paper. Suggest they choose a number to double to make an egg carton and figure out the total number of eggs it will hold. Help children select numbers for their egg cartons that they can handle. Some children may be interested in exploring large numbers (if they draw a carton with two rows of twelve, how many eggs would that be altogether?). Also, encourage children to try numbers that won't work (odd numbers) and ask them to explain their thinking about why no one makes egg cartons in those sizes. [See Figures 2 and 3]

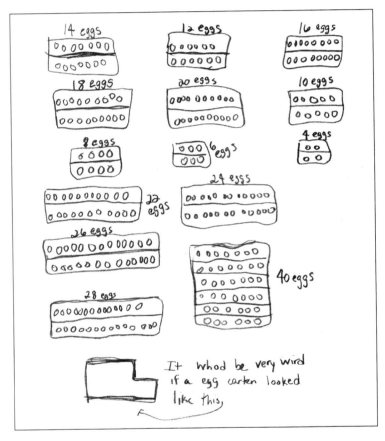

Figure 2

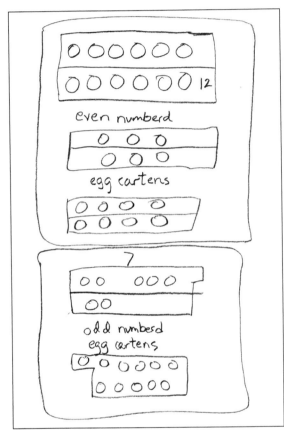

Figure 3

Preparing for the Math Congress

Ask children to make posters of their work and then conduct a "gallery walk" to give them a chance to review each other's posters.

Ask children to make posters of the containers they have designed. Display the posters around the room and have a gallery walk so that everyone gets a chance to see the various containers.

Facilitating the Math Congress

After the gallery walk, convene the class in the meeting area. Display a pocket hundred chart and have a few children place colored transparent inserts into the chart to highlight the sizes of all the containers they have made. Although not all the even numbers are likely to be marked, you will probably have enough of a variety to discuss predictions of other numbers that might be doubles. Encourage children to notice the patterns on the chart, such as the last digits (0, 2, 4, 6, and 8), the fact that the pockets with inserts often alternate, and the fact that they appear in columns. Take predictions of other numbers that might be doubles, checking them out if children are not sure, and continue adding colored transparent inserts. You can also refer the children to the doubles on the number line they made on Day Two.

☀ Use a pocket hundred chart to highlight the sizes of containers children made.

☀ Encourage children to notice the patterns that appear and to use those patterns to predict other numbers that might be doubles.

Reflections on the Day

Today the children had an opportunity to investigate doubling numbers further. You were able to look for evidence of which children are learning doubles, using these to find sums for near doubles, and making connections between contexts. When a context is strong enough, children will often begin to use it as a reference point. For example, the carton for a dozen eggs will remind some children of the book *Madeline* (the twelve little girls in two straight lines). As the results of doubling numbers were highlighted on a pocket hundred chart, children began to notice patterns. Today you established the terrain for the journey ahead.

Things That Come in Pairs—Shoes

Materials Needed

Class-size arithmetic rack

Student recording sheet for the shoe investigation (Appendix B)—one per child

Open number line from Day Two

Pocket hundred chart with highlighted numbers from Day Three

Large chart pad and easel

Markers

The day begins with a minilesson using a string of related problems crafted to continue supporting the automatizing of doubles and near doubles. A new context about shoes is then introduced to explore the relationship of doubles to skip-counting pairs—four pairs can be thought of as four sets of two (2, 4, 6, 8) or as two sets of four (4 + 4).

Day Four Outline

Minilesson: A String of Related Problems

☀ Show and discuss arrangements of beads on the arithmetic rack designed to support automatizing doubles and using doubles to solve near-doubles problems.

Developing the Context

☀ Introduce the shoe context and ask children to work on Appendix B.

Supporting the Investigation

☀ Note children's strategies and use the context to help them realize the meaning of what they are doing.

Preparing for the Math Congress

☀ Ask children to review their work and think about strategies they want to share in the math congress.

Facilitating the Math Congress

☀ Record children's data in a t-chart and discuss the doubling pattern that appears.

☀ Encourage children to draw connections to the numbers on the open number line and/or a pocket hundred chart.

Minilesson: A String of Related Problems (10–15 minutes)

Use the class-size arithmetic rack as you did on Day Three to do the following string. Show one problem at a time on the arithmetic rack. Each time you show an image, state the problem and ask for thumbs-up when children have an answer. Explore alternative strategies but encourage the children to make use of the relations in the string.

> ☀ Show and discuss arrangements of beads on the arithmetic rack designed to support automatizing doubles and using doubles to solve near-doubles problems.

String of related problems:

5 on the top, 5 on the bottom

6 on the top, 6 on the bottom

6 on the top, 5 on the bottom

8 on the top, 8 on the bottom

8 on the top, 9 on the bottom

7 on the top, 6 on the bottom

Developing the Context

Explain that you have been thinking about all the doubling the class has been doing and that now everywhere you look you see things that come in doubles. Ask the children if this is happening to them. (The purpose of this question is twofold: it develops the context and it also challenges the children to begin to mathematize their worlds.) Explain that last night you looked in your closet and you realized—shoes are perfect for thinking about doubles! Shoes come in pairs—and a pair is a double of one. Ask if any of the children upon entering their home take their shoes off and place them by the door. Explain that this is a common practice, for example, in many Asian families. Have children imagine with you all the pairs of shoes for a family lined up at the door. Next have them imagine a pair of shoes for each member in their own family. Distribute a recording sheet (Appendix B) to each child and ask them to make a drawing of each person's shoes and write down the number of people, the number of pairs of shoes, and the total number of shoes (single shoes).

Note: Be sure that you use a broad definition of family when asking the children to draw shoes for each family member. Children in your class may come from a variety of family structures. You can have children draw the shoes of all the people they live with and extended family members (grandparents, aunts, uncles, frequent visitors) as well.

Behind the Numbers

The solution to the first problem is likely to be known and can be used to solve the second by just adding two more. The first or second problem can be used to solve the third—supporting children in using known doubles to solve for unknown near doubles. The fourth problem might be difficult and many children may resort to counting by ones, but you can encourage them to think about doubles they know—for example, $(5 + 5) + (3 + 3)$. The color of the beads on the arithmetic rack makes these doubles stand out. The fourth problem can then be used to solve for the next, a near double. The last problem requires children to construct their own "helper" problems, such as $6 + 6$ or $7 + 7$.

> ☀ Introduce the shoe context and ask children to work on Appendix B.

Appendix B — Student recording sheet for the shoe investigation

Name _____ Date _____

■ There are _____ people in my family.
These are their shoes.

There are _____ pairs of shoes.

There are _____ single shoes.

Supporting the Investigation

☀ Note children's strategies and use the context to help them realize the meaning of what they are doing.

As children work, move around and confer and support their investigations as needed. Expect to see many children counting the shoes by ones. Others may use skip-counting by twos. Still others may realize that the number of people is just doubled.

Conferring with Children at Work

Inside One Classroom

Author's Notes

Daniel: I'm drawing John's shoes. He likes to wear sneakers. Then I'll make Peter's. His are black and shiny. *(He has already drawn four pairs and these two pairs will make six pairs.)*

Madeline (the teacher): I bet these are yours, right? *(Pointing to one of the pairs.)* They look like the ones you're wearing.

Madeline makes use of the context. Staying in the context helps children realize the meaning of what they are doing.

Daniel: Yep. They're new!

Madeline: How many people have you drawn shoes for so far?

Daniel: There's 1, 2, 3, 4, 5, 6. There's 6 people.

Madeline: I wonder how many shoes that will be?

Daniel: I'll count—2, 4, 6, 8, 10, 12.

Madeline checks first to see if Daniel realizes that the total number of shoes will be double. She notes the number of people that he needs to count, but that he is now skip-counting.

Madeline: Hmmm. You have 6 people, 6 pairs of shoes…and that made 12 shoes. That's interesting. That's one of our double numbers, isn't it?

Daniel: Yep—6 plus 6.

Madeline: That's right! I wonder if we could have known it would be 12 without counting?

By wondering aloud, Madeline offers an inquiry. This is actually quite a difficult question as it requires that the context be seen as six pairs of two as well as two sets of six (six right shoes and six left shoes).

Preparing for the Math Congress

☀ Ask children to review their work and think about strategies they want to share in the math congress.

After the children have had sufficient time to complete their work, ask them to prepare for a math congress. Ask them to look at the numbers on their recording sheets and to come prepared to share them, as well as anything about the numbers that they think is interesting and any helpful strategies they used and want to share.

Facilitating the Math Congress

Ask the children to sit in a circle in the meeting area. Have a chart pad set up to record the data. Go around the circle and have children report their results. Use a t-chart to record as shown below.

☀ Record children's data in a t-chart and discuss the doubling pattern that appears.

☀ Encourage children to draw connections to the numbers on the open number line and/or a pocket hundred chart.

Number of Pairs of Shoes	Total Number of Shoes
3	6
5	10
4	8

It is not necessary to add duplicates if children have done the same numbers, but the use of the chart and the reporting of results around the circle gives everyone a chance to check to see if answers are the same. If some children have incorrect results, review them by examining the drawings or by using the class-size arithmetic rack (pushing over one bead on top and one bead on the bottom at the same time to represent the pairs of shoes). Let the children notice the doubling pattern. If they don't notice it, point it out. Ask them to share their thinking about what the numbers in the pattern represent and why the numbers of shoes would also be a double—like the numbers on their open number line and/or those highlighted on a pocket hundred chart.

Inside One Classroom

A Portion of the Math Congress

Madeline (the teacher): So now we have a chart with all our findings. After mathematicians collect all their findings, they often put them on a chart like this. Then they step back and think, "Is there anything interesting here?" So, mathematicians, turn to the person next to you and talk about anything interesting you notice. *(After several moments of pair talk, Madeline resumes whole-group conversation.)* Ethan, what did you and Josie talk about?

Ethan: All the numbers of shoes are over here. *(Pointing to the open number line constructed on Day Two.)*

Madeline: Oh my goodness. Now that is an interesting thing to notice. Who else noticed that? *(Several hands go up.)* Why would that be happening, I wonder?

Author's Notes

Madeline models what mathematicians do. They look for patterns; they step back and wonder; they inquire; they generalize.

Ethan has noticed that all the answers are even numbers. For a young mathematician, this is an important observation.

continued on next page

continued from previous page

Sophie: Because you go 2, 4, 6. Like that…you skip-count.

Madeline: I did see a lot of you skip-counting today. Meg, may we use your picture to look at this? *(Meg says yes and Madeline displays her picture.)* How did you skip-count, Sophie? Show us on Meg's picture.

Sophie: I counted 2, 4, 6, 8. *(Four pairs of shoes are drawn and Sophie skip-counts, marking each pair.)*

Leah: Two shoes in every pair.

Josie: You can't get a different number…you would have a shoe missing.

Madeline: Tell us more about that, Josie.

Josie: If you go 2, 4, 5, the 5 would be for only one shoe. A shoe is missing.

Madeline: So our double numbers are numbers that go in twos. And the other numbers don't go in twos? One is missing? Actually, mathematicians have a name for these numbers. The ones that go in twos they call even numbers. The ones that don't go in twos they call odd numbers.

Josie: Yeah it would be odd. If you have 5 shoes, you know something is wrong. A shoe is missing.

Michael: Look. I just noticed something. On the hundred chart… it goes odd, even, odd, even…like that. It's a pattern.

Madeline: Wow. Another interesting observation! What wonderful mathematicians you are.

Madeline chooses Meg's picture because she has drawn the shoes in a row, making two paired lines of right and left shoes. This picture makes it easy for others to understand the skip-counting. It's possible that some children might notice that there are two rows of four as well.

Madeline introduces the terminology of odds and evens only after children have constructed the ideas for themselves.

▨ Assessment Tips

Continue to observe the counting strategies that children use: note who needs to count over and over again to be certain the amount is still the same; who is still counting by ones; who skip-counts. Which children seem able to explain clearly the relationship between pairing and doubling? In the minilesson, which children used the relationships in the string and which did not, instead solving each as a brand-new problem? Which children use known doubles to figure out unknown doubles and near doubles? You might find it helpful to make copies of the graphic of the landscape of learning on page 10, one for each child's portfolio. As you continue with the unit, you can color in the big ideas and strategies you see children developing. In a sense, you will be mapping their journeys, the paths they take as young mathematicians.

CJ's drawing shows an understanding of a 2 to 1 correspondence.

Daniel's drawing shows an understanding of how 6 pairs can also be seen as 6 + 6.

Reflections on the Day

Today, children further explored the relationship between doubling, pairing, and counting by twos. They related the numbers on their open number line (the doubles) to numbers that can be derived by skip-counting by twos. The terminology of even and odd numbers was introduced. In the minilesson, children continued to work on automatizing the facts, using doubles and near doubles.

Shoes and More Shoes

Materials Needed

Shoe billboards
(Appendixes C–G)

3"x 5" index cards—one
per child

Drawing paper—one
sheet per pair of children

Connecting cubes, teddy
bears, or other counters,
as needed

Open number line from
Day Two

Pocket hundred chart
with highlighted numbers
from Day Three

Copies of class roster (list
of children's first names
only), as needed

Large chart paper—one
sheet per pair of children

Large chart pad
and easel

Markers

The day begins with a minilesson using quick images—billboards of advertisements for shoes. Each image is crafted to support the automatizing of doubles and near doubles. Children then draw a picture of their own favorite shoes on an index card and the class explores how many shoes there are in the whole class.

Day Five Outline

Minilesson: Quick Images

* Show and discuss quick image "billboards" designed to support auto-matizing doubles and using doubles to solve near-doubles problems.

Developing the Context

* Have each child draw a picture of their favorite pair of shoes on an index card.
* Ask children to figure out how many shoes are drawn on the cards in total.

Supporting the Investigation

* Note children's strategies and encourage them to justify their thinking.

Preparing for the Math Congress

* Ask children to prepare posters of their work to share during the math congress.

Minilesson: Quick Images (10–15 minutes)

Ask the children if they have ever seen billboards for advertisements along the highway (or in other places). Tell them you have made some shoe billboards. But just as when you are in a car traveling and the car goes by the signs very fast, you are going to make the signs go by quickly, too—so fast that it will probably not be possible to count all the shoes. Suggest that now, because they know so much about doubles and pairs, they will have other ways to know how many shoes there are. Use Appendixes C through G. Show one at a time, moving it left to right as a quick image, then cover the image and ask children to share what they saw. Each time you show an image, ask, "How many shoes?" and "How do you know?" Invite discussion on several strategies. Support children in developing strategies to automatize doubles and to use doubles to figure out near doubles.

☀ Show and discuss quick image "billboards" designed to support automatizing doubles and using doubles to solve near-doubles problems.

Behind the Numbers

Amounts of two and three objects can usually be subitized—seen as a unit. The shoe billboards are arranged so that children will probably see pairs of shoes, and they will also know how many pairs, but because the image will go by quickly they will not be able to count the shoes. They will need to use the information they see to figure out how many shoes there are. Quick images use the constraint of brief time to challenge children who are still counting by ones to develop other strategies such as skip-counting, counting on, doubling, and using doubles to figure out near doubles.

Inside One Classroom

A Portion of the Minilesson

Madeline (the teacher): Here's the first billboard. *(Referring to Appendix C.)* Look closely. Billboards go by quickly. *(Moves it left to right).* How many shoes? And how do you know? *(Covers the billboard to hide the image.)* CJ?

CJ: I saw 7!—2, 4, 6 *(uses fingers to show the twos)* and 1 more. So there are 7 shoes!

Madeline: Who saw it like CJ? *(Several hands go up.)* Did anyone see it a different way? Leah?

Leah: I saw 3 and 3 and I knew that was 6...then 1 more.

Ethan: I saw 4 and 3. I counted on—5, 6, 7.

Author's Notes

Madeline shows the image only briefly, then covers it.

She invites a discussion on a variety of strategies.

continued on next page

continued from previous page

Madeline: Let's look. *(Shows the billboard again.)* Look at that. You are all right! Here's the 3 pairs and 1 that CJ saw, and here's the 3 and 3 and 1 that Leah saw. Up and down, Leah? And Ethan, did you see these 4 shoes and these 3? *(Writes on the chart paper:)*

$$7 = 2 + 2 + 2 + 1 = 3 + 3 + 1 = 4 + 3$$

OK. Let's do the next billboard. Ready?

The strategies are recorded as equivalent expressions.

Developing the Context

☀ Have each child draw a picture of their favorite pair of shoes on an index card.

☀ Ask children to figure out how many shoes are drawn on the cards in total.

After the minilesson, have children draw one more picture of shoes—their most favorite pair ever. Have them draw this picture (of just one pair of shoes) on an index card and put their name on the back of the card. Collect the index cards and count them with the children to establish that a card has been completed by every child in class. If you use an attendance chart as part of your morning routine, use it to establish how many children are in class today and that the number of index cards is the same. If you do not have a chart, you can have the children count off to establish the number in attendance. Then assign math partners and ask them to figure out how many shoes are drawn on the cards in total.

Supporting the Investigation

☀ Note children's strategies and encourage them to justify their thinking.

Explain to the children that there are many helpful tools available if they would like to use them, such as connecting cubes, a pocket hundred chart (with the even numbers highlighted), and the doubles on the open number line. Make copies of the class roster available too as some children may prefer to use that. Do not allow children to count the shoes on the cards. Instead, remind them of the wonderful, helpful strategies shared on Day Four and challenge them to figure out the correct answer.

Move around the room noting the strategies children are using. Sit with a few children and confer. Here are some strategies you will probably see:

✦ Using the class roster or the attendance chart and trying to count by twos. This may be a challenge as it requires a "two-for-one" strategy. There are no shoes to count, just people, and the numbers are much larger than what the class has dealt with before. Support the children in keeping track of the number, reminding them of what they said just before if they lose count. You might also remind them of the patterns they have noticed on other days, such as the last digits being 0, 2, 4, 6, and 8.

- Adding the number in attendance twice—for example, if there are 26 children in class, trying to calculate 26 + 26.

- Using the pocket hundred chart or the doubles posted on the open number line. Here children will need to keep track of what the number involved stands for. Six on the hundred chart is three pairs, for three children. Once again you will need to support children in keeping track. You might suggest a t-chart like the one used on Day Four.

As you confer, you will probably have many children asking you if their answer is correct. Do *not* tell them if they have the right answer until they can convince you that they do. By challenging them to justify their thinking, you are pushing them to develop certainty—the logical necessity so necessary to mathematicians. When mathematicians solve problems or craft proofs, they do not line up in front of the wise one to get their answer checked. They craft a proof with logic that is so convincing that others, after reading it, say it must be so!

Preparing for the Math Congress

After children have had sufficient time to complete their work, ask them to work on posters for a math congress to be held on Day Six. On their posters they should write what they think the answer is and how they know this answer is correct. Their posters should use pictures and/or words in such a way as to convince other children in the class that the solutions shown are correct.

☀ Ask children to prepare posters of their work to share during the math congress.

Reflections on the Day

Today constraints on counting one by one were provided by quick images, using index cards, and large numbers. The objective was to challenge children who are still counting by ones to use doubles or skip-count. The pictures on the index cards will be used on Day Six during the math congress. They will also be used for the Shoe Game on Day Six. (Note: Please read the next page for directions on how to make the game boards now, as you will need some preparation time to get them ready for Day Six.)

Directions for Making the Shoe Game Boards

Photocopy five or six copies of every pair of shoes drawn on the index cards. Color copies are especially nice but you may find this costly. Black-and-white copies are sufficient. With a pair of scissors cut around every shoe, taking care to keep the pairs together. Glue around twenty pairs of shoes on a piece of oaktag to make a track for a game board (as in Figure 4). The exact number of pairs is not important and boards can be different, but be sure that you have complete pairs and that the track looks as though it is a path of shoe prints. Cover the board with clear adhesive paper or laminate it. Make one board for every two or three children in your class.

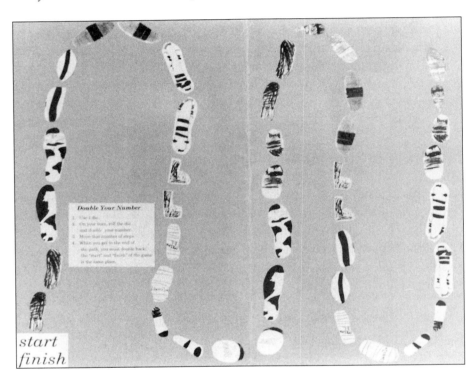

Figure 4

The Shoe Game

There is no minilesson today because time will be needed for the math congress on the work of Day Five and for the Shoe Game. After the game is introduced, children play in pairs or groups of three and then come back to the meeting area to discuss any interesting things they noticed.

Day Six Outline

Preparing for the Math Congress (continued from Day Five)

☀ Conduct a gallery walk to give children a chance to review each other's posters from Day Five.

☀ Plan to focus the congress discussion on posters that will encourage the progressive development of children's strategies.

Facilitating the Math Congress

☀ As posters are shared, encourage children to make sense of each other's strategies.

Developing the Context

☀ Model how to play the Shoe Game.

Supporting the Investigation

☀ Note children's strategies as they play the game and encourage them to notice and generalize the relationship between pairing and doubling.

Materials Needed

Children's posters from Day Five

Index cards with drawings of shoes from Day Five

Shoe Game game boards prepared on Day Five

Number cubes (with dots, one through six)—one per group of two or three children

Game pieces or counters—one per child

Preparing for the Math Congress (continued from Day Five)

- ☀ Conduct a gallery walk to give children a chance to review each other's posters from Day Five.

- ☀ Plan to focus the congress discussion on posters that will encourage the progressive development of children's strategies.

Display everyone's posters around the room, and have a brief gallery walk so that children can see the different ways their peers have written up their work to convince others that their solutions are correct.

■ Tips for Structuring the Math Congress

As you walk around, look for interesting pictures that are convincing. For example, a poster might have 26 pairs of shoes drawn (assuming that 26 children were in the class on Day Five) and then a circle may be drawn around the column of 26 right shoes and another around the column of 26 left shoes. On the side of the work might be written 26 + 26. A poster such as this shows both the pairs of shoes (the skip-counting) and the reason behind doubling the total number of children in the class. This is an especially important generalization for the young mathematicians in your class and thus if you have a poster like this it is important to discuss the idea. Another possibility is a poster that shows an emergent ratio table, like a t-chart. If any of the children have kept track of both pairs and shoes simultaneously, you might use their poster to discuss helpful ways to keep track. Whichever posters you choose should push the mathematical development of your community.

Facilitating the Math Congress

- ☀ As posters are shared, encourage children to make sense of each other's strategies.

After the gallery walk, convene a math congress in the meeting area to discuss a few of the posters. Have one or two pairs of children show their posters and discuss the related strategies and ideas.

A Portion of the Math Congress

Inside One Classroom

Madeline (the teacher): So many wonderful ideas posted! We have such a class of mathematicians! When you walked around, which posters did you see that helped you decide the answer? Was there one in particular that really convinced you?

Daniel: I like Sophie's and Leah's. It's pretty.

Madeline: It is pretty, isn't it? *(Sophie has drawn flowers on a lot of the shoes.)* When you looked at it, could you tell how many shoes will be in this pile of cards?

Author's Notes

Madeline continues to confirm that this is a community of young mathematicians. She asks, "Which arguments convinced you?" Even young children's drawings can be "mathematical arguments."

Often young children like a poster simply because of the color or layout. They need help learning to examine the mathematical argument presented on the poster.

continued on next page

continued from previous page

Daniel: Yep. I counted them. They had the same answer as me.

Madeline: So their poster convinced you because she drew the exact number of shoes, and she drew them in pairs. How many pairs did you make, Sophie?

Sophie: The same as the number of kids.

Madeline: Josh and CJ, your poster convinced me. You have the number of kids on yours too, and you wrote something interesting. You wrote 26 plus 26. Where did Josh and CJ get 26 plus 26? Can we tell from their poster? *(They have drawn every child with two shoes in front of each child.)*

The children are invited to examine each other's mathematics and to make sense of different ways of looking at the problem.

Yolanda: There's two shoes for every kid.

Josh: Yep. First one for every kid. That's 26. Then another for every kid. That's another 26.

Yolanda: Oh, I get it! Every kid gets two shoes. One and then another. That's so different than our way. We skip-counted. What made you think of plussing?

Developing the Context

After the math congress, ask the children to form a circle. Choose two children and play the Shoe Game with them in the center of the circle as a way to introduce the game and model how it is played.

☀ Model how to play the Shoe Game.

▦ Object of the Game

The purpose of the game is to automatize the doubles facts and to encourage children to examine the relationship between pairing and doubling that they have probably been discussing as the unit has progressed.

▦ Directions for Playing the Shoe Game

Children play in pairs or triads, depending on the number of boards you have made. Players take turns rolling a single number cube. They double the number that is shown and move a counter that many steps (single shoes) along the track. When they reach the end of the track, they double back to the beginning passing the other player in the opposite direction. Play ends when every player has returned to the starting point. Play is cooperative, not competitive.

Supporting the Investigation

☀ Note children's strategies as they play the game and encourage them to notice and generalize the relationship between pairing and doubling.

As children play the game, move around the room and sit with a few groups. Notice the strategies they are using. Do they know the double of the number shown on the cube automatically, or do they need to count the dots? You can use two number cubes for children who need help. After they roll the first cube, have them turn over the second cube to match the number on the first cube. As children play, you might challenge them to think about how it could be that when a number is rolled and then doubled, the number of pairs of shoes moved ends up being the same number as the number on the cube!

After children finish playing the game, ask them to return to the meeting area for a brief discussion of any interesting things they noticed or helpful strategies they used.

Conferring with Children at Work

Inside One Classroom

Madeline (the teacher): That's interesting. You know what I just noticed? Every time you roll a cube, you double it, right? And then you move that many spaces. So, Sadie, you rolled a 4 and moved 8 shoes, 4 plus 4. I noticed that it ended up being 4 pairs of shoes! The number on the roll matched the number of pairs of shoes. Look at that! Will that happen again?

Sadie: I don't think so.

Michael: My turn. *(Rolls a 3, moves 6 shoes.)*

Madeline: See, 3 pairs of shoes!

Sadie: It happened again!

Michael: That's weird.

Madeline: Hmmm. I wonder why that is happening.

Michael: Oh! I know! It's 3 right shoes and 3 left shoes. So it's 3 plus 3, but it's also 3 pairs of shoes!

Madeline: Wow…Michael, that is neat. Will you share what you've noticed and your ideas about it in the meeting area later?

Author's Notes

Madeline encourages the children to notice an important relationship.

She does not explain the relationship but challenges the children to consider its generalization.

Wondering aloud is a great way to model and encourage inquiry.

As a mathematician, Michael is given a chance to justify and explain his idea to the community.

Assessment Tips

As you walk around supporting children as they play the game, note which children need to count and which ones know the double without counting. Also note how the children determine the number on the cube. Are they counting each dot on the cube, or do they subitize the amount and count on? Are children noticing the relationship of doubled numbers to numbers that can be counted by twos (a case of the commutative property of multiplication, $2 \times n = n \times 2$)? It is helpful to jot down your observations on sticky notes. These can then be placed in the children's portfolios.

Reflections on the Day

Today children were encouraged in a math congress to justify how they knew the total number of shoes drawn on the index cards. This context was used to continue to support them in constructing an understanding of the relationship between pairing and doubling. These ideas were further supported with the Shoe Game. This game can now be added to your collection of math games and children can play it throughout the year.

Grandma's Necklaces

Materials Needed

Grandma's Necklaces
[If you do not have the full-color read-aloud book (available from Heinemann), you can use Appendix H.]

Large chart paper—three sheets

Student recording sheet for the necklace investigation (necklace #1) (Appendix I)—one per pair of children

Hundred chart (Appendix J)—one per pair of children

Drawing paper—a few sheets per pair of children

Pocket hundred chart with numerals and two colors of transparent inserts

Blue and green markers

A new context is introduced today with the story of *Grandma's Necklaces*. After listening to you read the story, the children set off to investigate what numbers of blue and green beads are needed to make necklaces like the ones in the story. This investigation will continue for the next four days of the unit. Today you will focus on the first necklace. Brief math congresses occur at the end of each day to help children along with their investigations. Data are shared and recorded on a hundred chart and some insights are discussed.

Day Seven Outline

Developing the Context

☀ Read *Grandma's Necklaces* and facilitate a discussion about other numbers that might work to make necklaces of the kind described in the story.

☀ Record children's predictions on chart paper.

Supporting the Investigation

☀ Note children's strategies as they investigate their predictions for necklace #1.

☀ Encourage children to draw pictures of the necklaces and to record their work on their recording sheets and hundred charts.

Preparing for the Math Congress

☀ Plan a congress discussion to highlight the patterns in the numbers children have been exploring.

Facilitating the Math Congress

☀ As children share numbers that worked and numbers that didn't, highlight the numbers on a pocket hundred chart and encourage children to consider the pattern that appears and generalize it.

Developing the Context

Gather the children in the meeting area and read the story, *Grandma's Necklaces*. When you have finished, reexamine the text to make sure that the children understand the patterns and the problems Mei-Lee ran into with 25 beads (13 blue and 12 green) and how 30 beads worked perfectly. Invite the children to offer their thoughts and to conjecture about other numbers that might work to make necklaces of the kind described in the story. What is the secret behind grandma's necklaces? What did the child in the story realize in her dream?

Display three pieces of chart paper, one for each necklace pattern. On the chart paper, make a list of some of the numbers the children think might work. Write down all numbers they offer. It is quite possible that a few children will suggest that all even numbers will work. Write that down on the chart paper for necklace #1. Ask if they think that this is true for all the necklace patterns. If they say yes, write this as a conjecture on all three sheets. Be careful not to acknowledge that it is correct for the first necklace. Mathematicians work to prove their conjectures. Over the next four days of the unit, your students will be immersed in trying a variety of numbers, collecting data, noticing patterns, and working to prove their ideas. Even if they easily see that the first necklace needs even numbers, they will probably be quite surprised to find that some of the numbers that worked for necklace #1 do not work for necklaces #2 and #3. It is the exhilaration of noticing patterns, offering conjectures, and proving one's ideas—figuring out why something works and being able to generalize it—that drives mathematicians. Don't deprive your students of this joy by making them feel that the task is to figure out an answer that you already know. Inquire with them. Model wonderment and the fun of doing mathematics!

After the context is fully developed, assign math partners and distribute blue and green markers, drawing paper, recording sheets (Appendix I) and hundred charts (Appendix J), explaining that today children should focus on necklace #1. Have them set to work investigating their predictions.

Supporting the Investigation

On this first day, concentrate on supporting your students in trying out different numbers, with a focus on necklace #1. Have them draw pictures of the necklaces, rather than string beads. Stringing beads can be tedious and children of this age often forget the pattern they are working on as they get distracted by the physical demands of the task. The drawings also constitute a record of the

☀ Read *Grandma's Necklaces* and facilitate a discussion about other numbers that might work to make necklaces of the kind described in the story.

☀ Record children's predictions on chart paper.

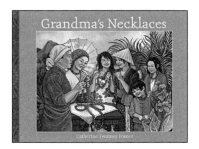

Behind the Numbers

There are three different necklaces in the story. All require even numbers of beads, and the number of blue beads must be equal to the number of green beads. The first necklace can be made with n sets of two (one of each color); the repeating unit is one blue bead and one green bead. As long as the numbers of blue and green beads are equal, any reasonable length using an even number of beads works. For example, the first necklace can be made with 10 beads, 12 beads, 14 beads, and so on, but not with an odd number of beads.

The second necklace is a bit more challenging; the repeating unit is five blue and five green, or ten beads. So although all possible numbers of beads for this type of necklace must be even (whatever the length), they must also be multiples of ten. For example, 20 works (two sets of 5 blue and 5 green) but 25 does not (because there would be 10 beads of one color together). The third necklace works only with even groups of three (which is the same as saying that only multiples of six will work). This investigation is designed to be very open-ended to allow you to differentiate. It is not expected that all children will solve all the necklace problems but there is much potentially rich math content here and you will want to devote ample time to this investigation.

☀ Note children's strategies as they investigate their predictions for necklace #1.

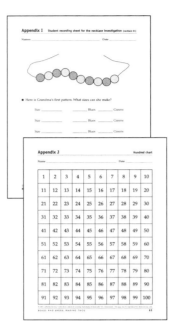

numbers of beads that worked and those that didn't. These records are important for promoting reflection. Explain that the drawings are drafts and allow for cross-outs and additions. Have the children record on both their recording sheets for necklace #1 and their hundred charts.

As you move around observing and conferring, you will probably see several strategies:

- ✦ Struggling to continue a pattern consistently. Although most of the children should be able to describe the pattern and verbally continue it, drawing it may be more difficult and they may need your support. Encourage them to verbally state the pattern of bead colors, and the number of each color, as they draw, and ask children to help each other.

- ✦ Trial and adjustment. Some children may randomly select numbers to try. When one doesn't work, they may add or remove beads to try to make the pattern fit. As you confer, encourage them to reflect on their adjustments and to make a list of the numbers that fit the pattern and the ones they had to fix. Encourage them to reflect on their results and not merely guess.

- ✦ Some children may quickly begin to see that for necklace #1, 15 beads of each color will work, as will 13, 14, and so on. Challenge the children to generalize. Does any number of beads work as long as *both* colors have the same number? Are the sizes that work numbers that are doubles (like on the open number line created on Day Two)? Is there a connection to the pairing, as with the shoes? Do only even numbers make the pattern work? Why not odd numbers?

- ✦ Given all the work of the previous week on doubles and pairing, some children may be able to provide a sound justification at the beginning of the day's work for concluding that only even numbers work. You can challenge them to explore the other necklace patterns.

Preparing for the Math Congress

After a sufficient amount of time has been devoted to the investigation, ask children to place all their work into their work folders and to come to the meeting area. Ask them to be prepared to tell what sizes they tried, which ones worked, and which ones didn't work. As children prepare, think over the strategies you have seen and the conjectures children have been making as they worked.

Facilitating the Math Congress

Use the two colors of transparent inserts for highlighting on a pocket hundred chart. Use one color for numbers that worked and one color for numbers that didn't. Have children share some of the drawings they made, the numbers that worked, and the numbers that didn't. Record the data with a pocket hundred chart. Challenge the children to generalize and relate the results to the work of the past week.

☀ As children share numbers that worked and numbers that didn't, highlight the numbers on a pocket hundred chart and encourage children to consider the pattern that appears and generalize it.

A Portion of the Math Congress

Inside One Classroom

Author's Notes

Madeline (the teacher)**:** So we found lots of numbers that worked, didn't we?

Nate: I think there is a pattern. It's gonna be every other one. Like before.

By marking the data on the hundred chart, children are encouraged to notice patterns.

Sophie: Yeah. Like when we walked in line.

The children begin to relate this context to the contexts of walking in line and shoes.

Madeline: What do you mean? Say more about that, Sophie. Are you noticing something about how the necklaces are related to walking hand in hand in line?

Sophie: Yeah. It's like the blue and green beads are holding hands. They go together, blue and green, blue and green.

Yolanda: It's like the shoes, too. The blue and green are like a pair of shoes. They go together, like Sophie said.

Madeline: So are you saying that only even numbers will work and that odd numbers won't work for this necklace?

Madeline challenges them to examine the relationships and to generalize.

Leah: Yes. Odd numbers can't work…like the shoes. You need a pair. If you have one extra, it's a problem. That's why Mei-Lee couldn't get 25 to work. She needed one more green. The greens have to be the same as the blues.

Madeline: Like our doubles?

Reflections on the Day

Children explored another doubling and pairing context today and related it to their previous work with doubles. On Day Eight children will work on the more challenging patterns of the other necklaces.

DAY EIGHT
The Second Necklace

Materials Needed

Grandma's Necklaces (Appendix H)

Charts from Day Seven listing conjectures about the three necklaces

Student recording sheet for the necklace investigation (necklace #2) (Appendix K)—one per pair of children

Hundred chart (Appendix J)—one per pair of children

Drawing paper—a few sheets per pair of children

Pocket hundred chart with numerals and two colors of transparent inserts

Blue and green markers

Today the class will explore the pattern of bead colors in the second necklace. The children are reminded of the pattern of this second necklace (five blue, five green), and they predict which numbers of each color of beads will work to make necklaces with different lengths, but the same pattern. Then they check whether their predictions will fit the conditions. A brief math congress is held at the end of the session.

Day Eight Outline

Developing the Context

* Revisit *Grandma's Necklaces* and discuss the pattern in the second necklace.
* Record children's conjectures about why certain numbers worked and other numbers didn't.

Supporting the Investigation

* Note children's strategies as they investigate their predictions for necklace #2.
* Encourage children to draw pictures of the necklaces and to record their work on their recording sheets and hundred charts.

Preparing for the Math Congress

* Plan to focus the congress discussion on the patterns in the numbers.

Facilitating the Math Congress

* As children share numbers that worked and numbers that didn't, highlight the numbers on a pocket hundred chart.
* Challenge children to generalize the results and draw connections to their work of the past week.

Developing the Context

Gather the children in the meeting area and reread the section of *Grandma's Necklaces* in which Mei-Lee tries to make a necklace with a pattern of five blue, five green. Or you may prefer to reread the whole story. Often children love to hear the story again. When you have finished, wonder aloud why the 25 beads didn't work for the second necklace but 30 did and remind children of the conjectures and predictions they made on Day Seven. Add any new conjectures to the charts and then assign math partners and distribute blue and green markers, drawing paper, recording sheets (Appendix K), and hundred charts (Appendix J), explaining that today children should focus on necklace #2. Have them begin working to investigate their predictions.

☀ Revisit *Grandma's Necklaces* and discuss the pattern in the second necklace.

☀ Record children's conjectures about why certain numbers worked and other numbers didn't.

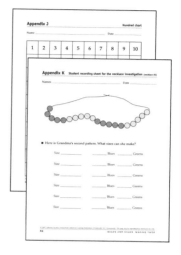

Supporting the Investigation

As you did on Day Seven, have children draw pictures of the necklaces, rather than string beads. Remind them that the drawings are drafts and that they shouldn't be afraid to cross out beads or fix necklaces that didn't fit the pattern. Have them record on the recording sheets and the hundred charts both the numbers of beads that worked and numbers that didn't. As you move around observing and conferring, you will probably see these strategies:

☀ Note children's strategies as they investigate their predictions for necklace #2.

☀ Encourage children to draw pictures of the necklaces and to record their work on their recording sheets and hundred charts.

✦ Trial and adjustment. Some children may randomly select numbers to try. When one doesn't work, they may add or remove beads to try to make the pattern fit. As you confer, encourage them to reflect on their adjustments and to make a list of the numbers that fit the pattern and the ones they had to fix. Encourage them to reflect on their results and not merely guess.

✦ Skip-counting by fives, making a list as they go and trying those numbers of beads. They will be surprised to find that not all multiples of five work. Encourage them to keep track of the number of groups of five that fit the pattern of necklace #2, or, if they have made a list of multiples as they skip-counted, to circle the ones that worked. They may also become intrigued with how necklaces made from some combinations of blue and green beads have a long string of beads of the same color, and others have one to four green beads that separate sets of blues. For example, 24 would be 5 blue, 5 green, 5 blue, 5 green, and 4 blue producing a string of 9 blue in a row when tied into a circle. On the other hand, 16 to 19 would have only one to four green beads between two sets of five blues when tied into a circle.

✦ Noting the pattern that occurs on the hundred chart, which shows that only multiples of ten work. Encourage children to consider why this is by asking how many groups of ten beads—five beads of each color—are in the necklaces that fit the pattern.

Preparing for the Math Congress

● Plan to focus the congress discussion on the patterns in the numbers.

After a sufficient amount of time has been spent on the investigation, ask children to place all their work into their work folders and to come to the meeting area prepared to tell what sizes they tried, which ones worked, and which ones didn't work. As children prepare, think over the strategies you have seen and the conjectures children have been making as they worked.

■ Tips for Structuring the Math Congress

Look for samples of work in which children have noticed that the numbers of beads in necklaces fitting the pattern have equal numbers of beads of each color and that these amounts increase in increments of five (10 blue and 10 green, 15 blue and 15 green, 20 blue and 20 green, etc.). Also look for samples in which children kept track of the number of groups of five (4 groups of five, 6 groups of five, 8 groups of five, etc.). Even numbers of groups of five work, but odd numbers of groups do not. In the congress, these two different ways of looking at the results will provide for an interesting conversation.

Facilitating the Math Congress

● As children share numbers that worked and numbers that didn't, highlight the numbers on a pocket hundred chart.

● Challenge children to generalize the results and draw connections to their work of the past week.

Use the two colors of the transparent squares for highlighting on a pocket hundred chart. As you did on Day Seven, use one color for numbers that worked and one color for numbers that didn't. Have children share some of the drawings they made, the numbers of beads of each color that fit the pattern, and the numbers that didn't. Record the data on a pocket hundred chart. As children recognize that the numbers that work are all multiples of ten (they may phrase this discovery as "the numbers you say when you skip-count by tens"), invite a few pairs of children to talk about the way they examined the reason the pattern appeared. Then challenge the children to generalize and relate the results to the work of the past week.

Inside One Classroom

A Portion of the Math Congress

Madeline (the teacher): So all the sizes that worked are in this column, 10, 20, 30, straight down here. Isn't this interesting! A few of you had some interesting ideas on this. Yolanda, would you tell us what you and Michael noticed?

Yolanda: We noticed that the beads…we skip-counted by fives. See 10 and 10, then 15 and 15, then 20 and 20. The blues and greens always have the same number. And it keeps going like that.

Author's Notes

By marking the data on the hundred chart, Madeline encourages the children to notice patterns.

The children are invited to present their ideas like mathematicians.

continued on next page

continued from previous page

Sophie: Hey! Like walking in line again! Every time the green gets 5 more, the blue does, too.

The children begin to relate this context to the contexts of walking in line and shoes.

Madeline: How many of you noticed what Yolanda is talking about? Does it make sense what Sophie just said?

Madeline presses the community to make sense of what each member says.

CJ: Yeah. It's like the blue and green beads are holding hands. They go together, blue and green, blue and green, but now there are 5 in each line.

Madeline: Daniel and Sadie, you kept track of the number of groups of five, didn't you? Tell us what you noticed and let's see if there is a connection here.

A second group shares a different but related idea.

Daniel: Yeah. There is. We noticed that 4 groups of five worked, then 6, then 8. The fives have to be even. Odd ones don't work.

Madeline: The number of groups has to be even?

Sadie: Yeah. Because they go together—5 greens and 5 blues.

Reflections on the Day

The second necklace investigation challenged children to consider not only even numbers, but even numbers of groups. This is a difficult idea for young children because here the group is being considered as a unit. The context is helping them realize the meaning of what they are doing; all the work of the previous week provided a strong foundation for this understanding. On Day Nine this work will be extended further as children consider the third necklace.

The Third Necklace

Materials Needed

Class-size arithmetic rack

Grandma's Necklaces **(Appendix H)**

Charts from Day Seven listing conjectures about the three necklaces

Student recording sheet for the necklace investigation (necklace #3) (Appendix L)—one per pair of children

Hundred chart (Appendix J)—one per pair of children

Drawing paper—a few sheets per pair of children

Pocket hundred chart with numerals and two colors of transparent inserts

Blue and green markers

Today begins with a minilesson, using the arithmetic rack and a string of related problems crafted to support the use of doubles to solve near-doubles problems. Today, however, compensation is the focus—turning two addends into a double. The third necklace is then investigated to provide children with another opportunity to consider the ideas that were emerging on Day Eight.

Day Nine Outline

Minilesson: A String of Related Problems

☀ Show and discuss arrangements of beads on the arithmetic rack designed to support using compensation.

Developing the Context

☀ Revisit *Grandma's Necklaces* and discuss the pattern in the third necklace.

☀ Record children's conjectures about why certain numbers worked and other numbers didn't.

Supporting the Investigation

☀ Note children's strategies as they investigate their predictions for necklace #3.

☀ Encourage children to draw pictures of the necklaces and to record their work on their recording sheets and hundred charts.

Preparing for the Math Congress

☀ Plan to focus the congress discussion on the patterns in the numbers.

Facilitating the Math Congress

☀ As children share numbers that worked and numbers that didn't, highlight the numbers on a pocket hundred chart.

☀ Challenge children to generalize the results and draw connections to their work with the second necklace.

Minilesson: A String of Related Problems (10–15 minutes)

Use the class-size arithmetic rack to do the following string. Show one problem at a time on the arithmetic rack. Each time you show an image, state the problem and ask for thumbs-up when children have an answer. Explore alternative strategies but encourage the children to make use of the relations in the string.

☀ Show and discuss arrangements of beads on the arithmetic rack designed to support using compensation.

String of related problems:

5 on the top, 5 on the bottom

4 on the top, 6 on the bottom

8 on the top, 8 on the bottom

7 on the top, 9 on the bottom

6 on the top, 6 on the bottom

7 on the top, 5 on the bottom

6 on the top, 8 on the bottom

Behind the Numbers

The numbers in the problems were carefully chosen. Children probably just know the solution to the first problem. The numbers in the second problem can be turned into the numbers from the first. It is not likely that children will think of this, but when the answer produced is the same you have a chance to explore why. Slide one bead away from the group of six, and add one bead to the group of four to help them consider why the answers are the same. The next four problems are in two sets of pairs, crafted to support the same strategy—compensation. The last problem requires children to make their own "helping" double.

Developing the Context

After the minilesson, reread the section of *Grandma's Necklaces* in which Mei-Lee tries to make a necklace with a pattern of three blue, three green. Explain that today this third necklace will be the focus of the investigation. Remind children of the conjectures and predictions they made on the charts prepared on Day Seven. Invite new predictions and add them to the charts. Assign math partners and distribute green and blue markers, drawing paper, recording sheets (Appendix L) and hundred charts (Appendix J) to each pair of children. Have them begin working to investigate their predictions.

☀ Revisit *Grandma's Necklaces* and discuss the pattern in the third necklace.

☀ Record children's conjectures about why certain numbers worked and other numbers didn't.

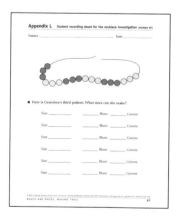

Supporting the Investigation

As you did on previous days, have children draw pictures of the necklaces, rather than stringing beads. Remind them that the drawings are drafts and that they shouldn't be afraid to cross out beads or fix necklaces that don't work. Have them record on the hundred charts and recording sheets both the numbers of beads that worked and those that didn't. As you move around observing and conferring, you will probably see these strategies:

+ Trial and adjustment. Some children may randomly choose numbers to try. When one doesn't work, they may add or remove beads to try to make the pattern fit. As you confer, encourage children to reflect on their adjustments and to make a list of the numbers that fit the pattern and the ones they had to fix. Encourage them to reflect on their results and not merely guess.

☀ Note children's strategies as they investigate their predictions for necklace #3.

☀ Encourage children to draw pictures of the necklaces and to record their work on their recording sheets and hundred charts.

+ Skip-counting by threes, making a list as they go and trying those sizes. Children will be surprised to find that not all multiples of three work. Remind them of what happened with the fives on Day Eight and encourage them to keep track of the number of groups of three that work or, if they have made a list of multiples as they skip-counted, to circle the ones that worked. They may also become intrigued with how necklaces made from some combinations of blue and green beads have a long string of beads of the same color, and others have just one or two green beads that separate the blues.

+ Noting that once again the numbers of beads of each color must be the same. The totals (the size) are doubles. Encourage children to consider how the number of beads of each color increases by three while the total increases by six when the length of the necklace is increased.

Preparing for the Math Congress

☀ Plan to focus the congress discussion on the patterns in the numbers.

After a sufficient amount of time has been spent on the investigation, ask children to place all their work into their work folders and to come to the meeting area prepared to tell what sizes they tried, which ones worked, and which ones didn't work. As children prepare, think over the strategies you have seen and the conjectures children have been making as they worked.

▦ Tips for Structuring the Math Congress

As you did on Day Eight, look for samples of work in which children noticed that the numbers of beads in necklaces fitting the pattern have equal numbers of beads of each color and that these numbers increase in increments of three (6 blue and 6 green; 9 blue and 9 green; 12 blue and 12 green, etc.). Also look for samples in which children kept track of the number of groups of three (4 groups of three, 6 groups of three, 8 groups of three, etc.). Even numbers of groups of three work, but odd numbers of groups do not. In the congress these two different ways of looking at the results will provide for an interesting conversation, just as they did on Day Eight. At this point some children may realize that odd numbers of groups of five and three (that is, an even number of groups of one color and an odd number of groups of the other color) result in a break in the pattern and that the total number of groups must be even because there are two colors.

Facilitating the Math Congress

Use the two colors of the transparent squares for highlighting on a pocket hundred chart. As you did on previous days, use one color for numbers that fit the pattern and one color for numbers that didn't. Have children share some of the drawings they made, the numbers of beads that worked, and the numbers that didn't. Record the data on a pocket hundred chart. Invite a few pairs of children to talk about their findings and challenge the children to generalize and relate the results to the groups of five on Day Eight.

☀ As children share numbers that worked and numbers that didn't, highlight the numbers on a pocket hundred chart.

☀ Challenge children to generalize the results and draw connections to their work with the second necklace.

Reflections on the Day

In today's minilesson, children were encouraged to use doubles as a way to automatize the addition facts. The third necklace investigation provided children with another opportunity to consider a group as a unit and to realize that an even total number of groups was needed because there are two colors in Grandma's necklaces.

Grandma's Special Numbers

Materials Needed

Class-size arithmetic rack

Grandma's Necklaces (Appendix H)

Pocket hundred chart with numerals and three colors of transparent inserts (remove the transparent inserts from Day Nine)

Hundred chart (Appendix J)—one per pair of children

Drawing paper—a few sheets per pair of children

Children's work from Days Seven, Eight, and Nine

Blue and green markers

Large chart pad and easel

Today provides children with a chance to consolidate what they have been learning as they progressed through this unit. In the minilesson they continue to look at how helpful doubles can be in automatizing the basic facts. In the subsequent investigation they examine the numbers that worked for all the necklaces and they investigate to find more of "Grandma's special numbers." A culminating math congress is held and several important generalizations about Grandma's special numbers are discussed and charted.

Day Ten Outline

Minilesson: A String of Related Problems

☀ Show and discuss arrangements of beads on the arithmetic rack designed to support using compensation.

Developing the Context

☀ Use a pocket hundred chart to highlight the numbers (up to 30) that work for each necklace and discuss how only one number thus far works for all three necklaces.

☀ Ask children to investigate other numbers that might work for more than one necklace.

Supporting the Investigation

☀ Encourage children to explain their predictions and generalize their findings.

Preparing for the Math Congress

☀ Plan to focus the congress discussion on the patterns in the numbers.

Facilitating the Math Congress

☀ Use a pocket hundred chart to highlight more numbers that worked and then to explore the generalizations children share.

Minilesson: A String of Related Problems (10–15 minutes)

Use the class-size arithmetic rack to do the following string. Show one problem at a time on the arithmetic rack. Each time you show an image, state the problem and ask for thumbs-up when children have an answer. Explore alternative strategies but encourage the children to make use of the relations in the string.

☀ Show and discuss arrangements of beads on the arithmetic rack designed to support using compensation.

String of related problems:

5 on the top, 5 on the bottom

4 on the top, 6 on the bottom

3 on the top, 7 on the bottom

8 on the top, 8 on the bottom

9 on the top, 7 on the bottom

7 on the top, 5 on the bottom

6 on the top, 8 on the bottom

Developing the Context

Remind children of the many wonderful ideas they had as they worked to examine Grandma's necklaces. Use one color transparent square for the first necklace and invite the children to tell you what sizes worked. Highlight these numbers on a pocket hundred chart. Just go up to 30. Next, use a different color to highlight the answers that the children found for the second necklace. Again, just go up to 30. Use a third color for the sizes that worked for the third necklace, and, again, just go up to 30. Now you have a chart that shows why Grandma said, "You have to think about the numbers. Only some numbers work." Some numbers work for only one necklace; some work for two necklaces; and only one number thus far, 30, works for all three necklaces. Now children know why 30 was one of Grandma's "really special numbers." Invite predictions for other "really special numbers" that might work for more than one necklace. Distribute fresh copies of the hundred chart (Appendix J) and children's work from the past few days, assign math partners, and let them get to work!

Behind the Numbers

Children probably just know the solution to the first problem. The numbers in the second problem can be changed into the numbers in the first. It is not likely that children will think of this, but when the answer produced is the same you have a chance to explore why. As you did on Day Nine, slide one bead away from the group of six, and add one bead to the group of four to help them consider why the answers are the same. The solution to the third problem is also equivalent to those of the first and second. The problems in the string are crafted to support the same strategy as on Day Nine—compensation. The use of doubles can often be very powerful. Find the midpoint between two addends and double it! The last several problems in the string require children to make their own "helping" double.

☀ Use a pocket hundred chart to highlight the numbers (up to 30) that work for each necklace and discuss how only one number thus far works for all three necklaces.

☀ Ask children to investigate other numbers that might work for more than one necklace.

Supporting the Investigation

☀ Encourage children to explain their predictions and generalize their findings.

As you did on previous days, have children draw pictures of the necklaces. But today try to find moments to push for generalizations. As children work with greater numbers, encourage predictions and explanations for the predictions. A lack of knowledge of the names of the numbers they are trying to count may be a hurdle for some. Help them count. This is a meaningful context for children to experience counting greater numbers.

After enough time has been spent on the investigation, ask children to place all their work into their work folders and to come to the meeting area to talk about the special numbers they found.

Behind the Numbers

There are several nice generalizations children can make. Any number that works for the second necklace also works for the first necklace (because all multiples of ten are even). Any number that works for the third necklace also works for the first necklace (because any multiple of six is even). Only even numbers work because there are two colors with equal numbers of beads needed. There are many more numbers that work for the first necklace than for any of the others, and the third necklace has the fewest. For a number to work for all three necklaces, it must be a multiple of six, ten, and two. A few children may be able to find 60 and 90 through trial and adjustment or skip-counting, and one or two may even conjecture 120. It is not important that children find all of these "special numbers." Multiples and numbers this large are far beyond the scope of what is expected in the early grades. Even skip-counting can be a major challenge.

Consider this an opportunity for differentiation. Children who are challenged by dealing with small numbers can work further on necklaces with few beads, revisiting the ideas that have been discussed during the week. Others may be able to extend what they have been doing and you can support them in making generalizations you feel they can handle. Don't underestimate your students. They may surprise you!

Conferring with Children at Work

Inside One Classroom

Daniel: We're making large necklaces, the ones that people can loop lots of times. We think 100 beads will work!

Madeline (the teacher): Wow. That is a long necklace. Which patterns do you think it will work for?

continued on next page

Author's Notes

Madeline starts with the number they chose—100. But she encourages them to predict rather than to draw right away.

continued from previous page

Brian: Maybe the first one. I know how to write 100. It ends in zero. I think it will be a double.

Madeline: And the first necklace works with double numbers?

Good questions cause children to reflect on what they are doing and saying.

Brian: Yep. Remember blue and green have to be the same number.

Madeline: That's right. I remember now. I wonder what that amount will be? What number doubled will be 100?

Daniel: Hey! I know—50 and 50 make 100!

Brian: Yeah! It works for the blue-and-green pattern—50 blue beads and 50 green!

Madeline: Wow. You are good thinkers! Now you don't even have to draw that one! What about the second necklace? Can you make the second necklace in the size of one hundred?

Madeline's question causes them to reflect and generalize. Now they do not need to draw.

Brian: Yeah. Hey, that works, too. 'Cause 10, 20, 30, 40 …see on the hundred chart. If you count by tens you land on 100.

Madeline: Hmm. I'm noticing that if you count by tens you always land on numbers that end with a zero, see? *(Pointing to the hundred chart.)* Does this mean that all of these numbers that work for the second necklace also work for the first necklace?

Madeline challenges the children to generalize.

Brian: Yeah. Wow. These are all special. *(Pointing to the multiples of ten.)* But I don't know if they work for the third necklace. Because 20 didn't. And we tried 40 and that didn't either. Let's try 100. I'll draw it. *(Draws the 3 blue, 3 green pattern up to 43, loses count, and starts counting again. This time he adds a few more counting on, but at 47 he loses count again.)*

Madeline: This is hard, isn't it? I have an idea. Why don't you get a pencil and mark 10, then 20, then 30, and keep marking like that. Then you would know what you have counted and you wouldn't have to start over each time.

It is difficult to draw beads and count at the same time. Madeline encourages them to keep track by marking tens.

Daniel: Yeah. Good idea. *(Uses a pencil to mark the decades as they work. Soon they reach 59.)* What comes after 59?

Madeline: Let's look on the hundred chart. Here's 59. Next is 60.

Daniel: OK—60. Hey, 60 works!

As children begin to construct an understanding of the number system, the sequence of ones between the decades, 1–9, is often easier for children to name than the turning points of the decades. Madeline refers Daniel to the hundred chart and helps him find 59. She names 60 and then challenges again.

Madeline: Wow, look at that. It does! You found another really special one! The number 60 works for all the necklaces! Do you think you'll find another before you get to 100?

Preparing for the Math Congress

☀ Plan to focus the congress discussion on the patterns in the numbers.

It is helpful to get more answers up on the pocket hundred chart so that the patterns on it can be used as the discussion continues. For this reason, plan on starting the congress with children sharing their discoveries of numbers they found that worked and use the three colors of the transparent squares to mark them on the hundred chart. Then start a discussion on the generalizations.

Facilitating the Math Congress

☀ Use the pocket hundred chart to highlight more numbers that worked and then to explore the generalizations children share.

Continue as you began before children began to work, using the three colors of the transparent squares and the hundred chart to mark more of the numbers as children share. Once the results are up, have a few children share some of the important generalizations they have been discussing. Record them on large chart paper. Children might offer the following generalizations:

- ✦ Any number that works for the second necklace also works for the first necklace.
- ✦ Any number that works for the third necklace also works for the first necklace.
- ✦ Only even numbers work because there are two colors with equal numbers of beads needed. Odd total numbers of beads don't work for any of Grandma's patterns.
- ✦ There are many more numbers that work for the first necklace than for any of the others, and the third necklace has the fewest possible numbers.
- ✦ For a number to work for the first necklace, you have to land on it when you skip-count by twos.
- ✦ For a number to work for the second necklace, you have to land on it when you skip-count by tens.
- ✦ For a number to work for the third necklace, you have to land on it when you skip-count by sixes.
- ✦ For a number to work for all three necklaces (the very special numbers), you have to land on it when you skip-count by twos and tens and sixes.
- ✦ If you skip-count by thirties, you get all the really special numbers.

Children may express these ideas in their own words in different ways, but be alert for the moments to support them in generalizing. Maximize the moments and use the hundred chart to explore and check out their ideas.

◼ Assessment Tips

Collect all the work completed today and make notes regarding the children's approaches as they explored Grandma's necklaces. Compare the work of today to that done on Day Nine and the days before. Think about your congress and the generalizations children made about number. Note further growth and development in their understanding of even and odd numbers, their counting strategies, and their use of doubles in solving near doubles as they work to automatize the basic facts. Use the graphic of the landscape of learning and continue to map out children's pathways. Now do you have evidence for everyone?

To help your students reflect back on the ideas they have constructed as this unit progressed, make a class display—a sociohistorical wall—documenting the progression of the unit and an explanation of the important ideas constructed over the past two weeks. Use samples of children's drawings and a description of some of the ideas and strategies they tried. Add the chart of generalizations you made in the last math congress. By making this display available, you allow your class to revisit and reflect on all the wonderful ideas and strategies constructed throughout the unit.

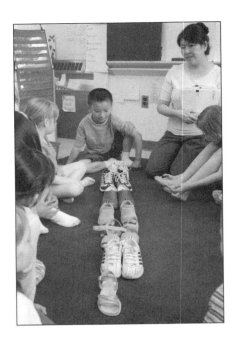

Reflections on the Unit

The mathematician Reuben Hersh once said, "It's the questions that drive mathematics. Solving problems and making up new ones is the essence of mathematical life. If mathematics is conceived apart from mathematical life, of course it seems—dead" (1997, page 18). With this unit, children were encouraged to inquire, to interpret data, to organize their results, and to construct ideas about even and odd numbers. They worked to automatize doubles and use them in clever ways to solve for near doubles. They were supported in envisioning the world around them with a mathematical lens as they explored lines of objects, containers that hold doubles, pairs of shoes, and the patterns in bead necklaces. When mathematics is understood as mathematizing one's world, it becomes creative and alive. And children, in learning to mathematize their lived worlds, will come to see mathematics as the living discipline it is, with themselves a part of an innovative, constructive mathematical community, hard at work.

■ To make a class-size arithmetic rack, find a large piece of cardboard, about three feet by one and a half feet. Punch four holes, two on each side, through the cardboard, approximately six inches apart top to bottom, but two feet across. Using wire or thin rope (such as clothesline), string twenty beads in two rows of ten each (five of each color) as in the illustration below. Thread the wire or rope through the holes and twist or tie in the back. *[Note: If you use wire, it is possible to use connecting cubes in place of beads]*

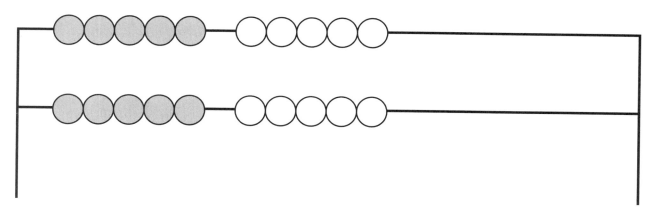

Rows are approximately six inches apart (top to bottom) and two feet long

For information on where to purchase an arithmetic rack, visit www.contextsforlearning.com.

Name _____ Date _____

■ There are _____ people in my family.

These are their shoes.

There are _____ pairs of shoes.

There are _____ single shoes.

BEADS AND SHOES, MAKING TWOS

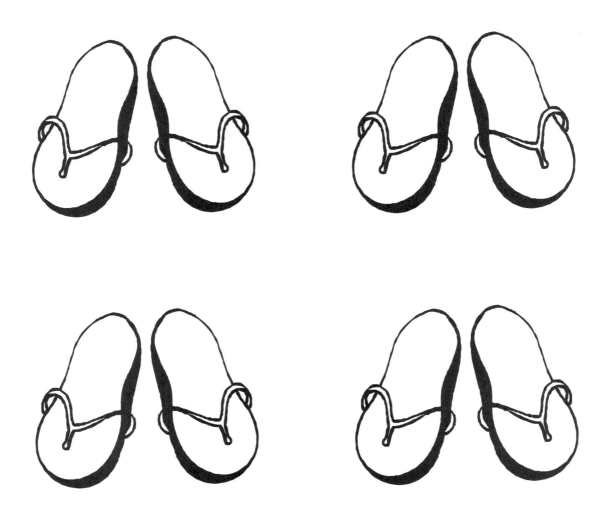

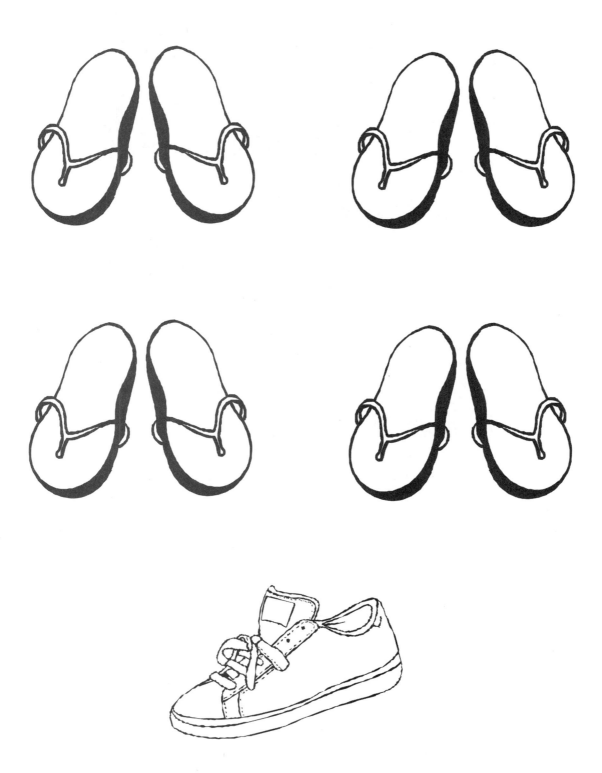

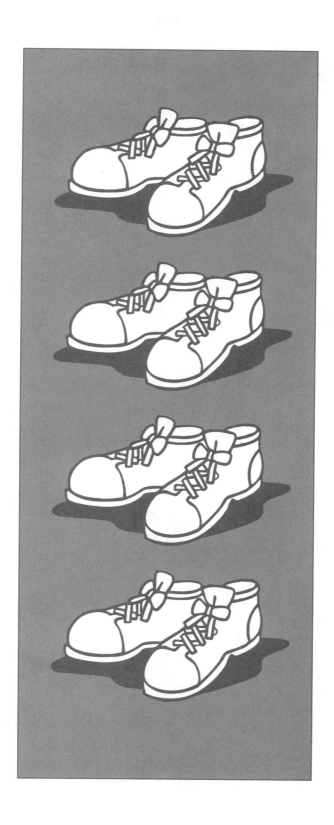

A long, long time ago, when my grandma was a little girl, she made very special glass bead necklaces. Some of the beads were a deep, deep blue like the ocean. My grandma would go to the fields and hold these in the sun. They would glisten and twinkle like diamonds and silver and you could see the blue of the sky and the violets of the fields in them.

My grandma had other beads, too. She called these her glimmering greens. In the day they were turquoise and aqua but at night they became the deep, deep green of the forest. My grandma said if you held the glimmering greens just above the water at sunset in the lagoon where the sea was very calm you could see all the colors of little fish swimming in them.

My grandma was known far and wide for her necklaces. People walked over mountains and traveled for days to get to the village where my grandma lived—just to see the beautiful glass bead necklaces.

But it wasn't just the beautiful beads that made the necklaces famous. My grandma could make special patterns with the beads. First, she would use a deep blue one. Then she would carefully push the thin silvery needle with the special string through a glimmering green one. Then a blue one again, and then another green. Blue, green, blue, green—my grandma was making a pattern.

Appendix H

Sometimes my grandma would make a different pattern: five blues, then five greens, then five blues, then five greens . . . Or sometimes she would use three blues and three greens, and then repeat that.

My grandma made her necklaces in lots of sizes, too. Some necklaces were really long and people would twist them and wear them in many loops. Some were middle-sized. These could be worn in single loops. Sometimes my grandma would make little ones for the children.

Lots of people in the village tried to make necklaces, too. My grandma told me that one day her cousin, Mei-Lee, found twenty-five beautiful beads—thirteen deep blue ones and twelve glimmering green ones—and decided to use them to make a necklace. First, she tried the blue-green pattern. Blue, green, blue, green . . . She worked quickly and soon she was almost done. "Twenty-four. One bead left to go," Mei-Lee thought, "and soon I will be famous just like my cousin." She placed the last bead on the string and tied it. Then she realized something had gone wrong. The pattern didn't work! She had two blue beads together!

It took Mei-Lee a long time to take all the beautiful beads off the string because she wanted to be careful not to lose any. Finally she was done and ready to start a new necklace. "I'll try the five and five pattern," Mei-Lee thought. "That pattern should work because twenty-five has a five at the end." And so she started all over with five blue beads together and then five greens. Five blue, five green, five blue . . . . "This time it will work, I'm sure. My necklace will be beautiful and I will be famous," Mei-Lee thought. All the groups of fives were looking so pretty. But something went wrong again. When Mei-Lee placed the twentieth bead on the string she had three blue and two green beads left! "This is so strange," Mei-Lee thought. "How did I get more blue beads? Or did I lose some green beads?" She counted the beads very carefully. There were still twenty-five—exactly.

Very carefully she took all twenty-five beads off the string, one by one. She put all the blue beads in a pile and counted them—thirteen. Next she put the glimmering green ones in a pile and counted them—twelve. Mei-Lee was puzzled. "All right, I'll try the three blue and three green pattern," Mei-Lee thought. "Maybe twenty-five is the perfect amount for that pattern." Three blue, three green, three blue . . . She kept going, working very hard. She wanted so much to be famous like her cousin, but she was becoming very tired. Finally, she was at twenty-four. The necklace looked really pretty so far and soon she would be done! But then Mei-Lee realized she had only one bead left, and it was blue. This pattern wouldn't work either! When she put the last bead on and tied the string, she had four blue beads together!

When my grandma told me the story about Mei-Lee, she was laughing. And then she leaned over and whispered in my ear, "You see, it's not just the beads that are special. The numbers are, too. You have to think about the numbers. Only some numbers work." I thought and thought about what my grandma meant. Why would the numbers matter?

That night I got my crayons out and drew many pictures of necklaces. I tried lots and lots of different numbers. I made big necklaces and little necklaces . . . and lots of different middle-sized ones. My grandma was right! Some numbers worked and some didn't. And some numbers that worked for the blue-green pattern didn't work for the other patterns. What a puzzle!

That night I dreamed of the deep blue glass beads like the ocean and the glimmering green ones with the fish swimming in them. My grandma was washing them in the lagoon so they would glisten. Around her feet were numerals and the waves were washing them gently to shore. First a two, then a four, then a six . . . And it was then that I knew. I woke up with a start and I knew. Numbers have patterns, too! I knew the secret of the glass bead necklaces! I ran downstairs to tell my grandma. I whispered in her ear the secret and she smiled a big, big smile.

"Does thirty work?" she asked me with her eyes twinkling.

"Yes!" I said. "Thirty is one of the really special numbers. It works for all the patterns. And I know some others that work, too!"

And then my grandma took me by the hand and led me into her room and showed me a very old wooden box with silver mermaids painted on it. She opened it and took out a long necklace made with the beautiful glass beads. "I have just one necklace left," she said, "and I have been saving it for you. It is very old and special so you must take very good care of it."

Then she gently placed the beautiful glass bead necklace around my neck. There were exactly thirty beads, fifteen deep blue ones like the ocean and fifteen glimmering green ones like the forest. And I could see the blue of the sky with the violets of the fields and all the colors of the fish swimming in the glass.

Appendix I   Student recording sheet for the necklace investigation (necklace #1)

Names _____   Date _____

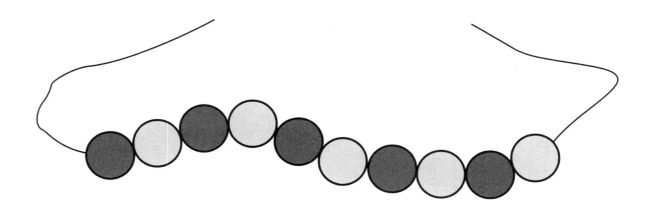

■ Here is Grandma's first pattern. What sizes can she make?

Size _____   _____ Blues _____ Greens

Size _____   _____ Blues _____ Greens

Size _____   _____ Blues _____ Greens

Size _____   _____ Blues _____ Greens

Size _____   _____ Blues _____ Greens

Size _____   _____ Blues _____ Greens

Name _____ Date _____

1	2	3	4	5	6	7	8	9	10
11	12	13	14	15	16	17	18	19	20
21	22	23	24	25	26	27	28	29	30
31	32	33	34	35	36	37	38	39	40
41	42	43	44	45	46	47	48	49	50
51	52	53	54	55	56	57	58	59	60
61	62	63	64	65	66	67	68	69	70
71	72	73	74	75	76	77	78	79	80
81	82	83	84	85	86	87	88	89	90
91	92	93	94	95	96	97	98	99	100

Appendix K Student recording sheet for the necklace investigation (necklace #2)

Names _____ Date _____

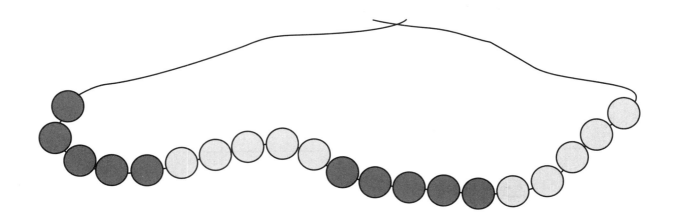

■ Here is Grandma's second pattern. What sizes can she make?

Size _____   _____ Blues _____ Greens

Size _____   _____ Blues _____ Greens

Size _____   _____ Blues _____ Greens

Size _____   _____ Blues _____ Greens

Size _____   _____ Blues _____ Greens

Size _____   _____ Blues _____ Greens

BEADS AND SHOES, MAKING TWOS

Names _____ Date _____

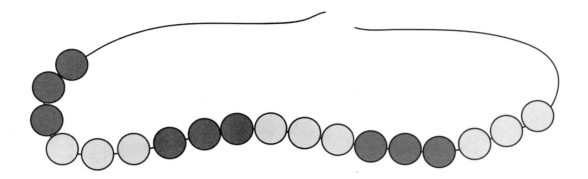

■ Here is Grandma's third pattern. What sizes can she make?

Size _____   _____ Blues _____ Greens

Size _____   _____ Blues _____ Greens

Size _____   _____ Blues _____ Greens

Size _____   _____ Blues _____ Greens

Size _____   _____ Blues _____ Greens

Size _____   _____ Blues _____ Greens